DOWN,

but not out

10 STEPS
FOR REBUILDING YOUR LIFE, YOUR CAREER,
& ALL THAT OTHER STUFF

DOWN,

but not out

10 STEPS
FOR REBUILDING YOUR LIFE, YOUR CAREER,
& ALL THAT OTHER STUFF

BARRY MINKOW

NELSON BOOKS
A Division of Thomas Nelson Publishers
Since 1798

www.thomasnelson.com

Published by Nelson Current, a division of Thomas Nelson, Inc., P.O. Box 141000, Nashville, Tennessee, 37214.

Library of Congress Cataloging-in-Publication Data

Minkow, Barry.
    Down, But Not Out: 10 Steps for Rebuilding Your Life, Your Career, & All That Other Stuff / Barry Minkow.
        p. cm.
    Includes bibliographical references and index.
    ISBN 1-59555-071-2 (alk. paper)
    1. Failure (Psychology) 2. Success. 3. Conduct of life. 4. Minkow, Barry.
I. Title.
    BF575.F14M56 2006
    158.1—dc22

2006033347

Printed in the United States of America

07 08 09 10 11 QW 5 4 3 2 1

To all who have fallen and failed, great or small.

CONTENTS

Introduction

FALLING SHORT

As a child I loved to play the game Simon Says. Think back for a moment . . . you remember: "Simon says raise your right hand. Simon says raise your left hand. Raise your right leg." And if you raised your right leg, do you remember what happened? You were out.

That is why I wrote this book. There are people who have failed in business, fallen to addiction, failed in a marriage, fallen short as a parent or even as a student, failed to make it as an athlete, or fallen morally. Some feel like they are in a bad Simon Says game—they feel that because they have failed, they are out!

But Simon was wrong. Although you may in fact be down, failing does *not* mean you are out. OK, so maybe you haven't been convicted of fraud, served time in jail, or been ordered to pay restitution (like I have). I am one of the few and not so proud. Regardless, even if the former isn't true about you it certainly doesn't exempt you from failure. What *is* true about every person who has failed? It is all about *you.*

Webster defines failure as "a lack of success . . . a failing in business: bankruptcy . . . one who has failed or is *falling short*" (emphasis mine). I'd like to home in on the phrase *falling short* because it is there we can all find common ground:

Falling short in business. You raised money from friends and relatives, people believed in you, and now—*poof!* That business is gone, along with the investment capital. As a result, those relationships may appear as if they will never be the same again.

Falling short because of addiction. Gambling, alcohol, prescription drugs, or even steroids can be the cause—but the effect has been devastating. Although a well-kept secret for years, through a strange set of circumstances your addiction has been revealed, and you are convinced your life is a failure.

Falling short in ethics. Maybe you violated a position of trust. Or, you worked for years to build up a solid reputation only to have it destroyed by a decision that, although not illegal, was certainly unethical, and it has cost you your reputation. It may take many more years to regain your former status.

Falling short in marriage. Only those of us who have experienced the pain of divorce can attest to the devastating emotions that go hand in glove with the death of a marriage. Your confidence is shattered by having the person closest to you desire a permanent separation. After all, if you were such a good person, why would your spouse want to leave?

Falling short as a parent. Too many long hours at the office in pursuit of success have left a void at home. It haunts you today, especially considering the fact that you were warned.

You once heard someone ask the rhetorical question, "When is the best time to get to know your fifteen-year-old?" and the answer was "When he or she is two!" But for some reason it did not sink in, and you continued to sacrifice that extraordinary relationship simply to get ahead. You are not alone.

Falling short in athletics. You didn't make the cut despite years of training. You've poured your life into a particular sport to the extent that you actually became identified with it. Whenever you went to a social event or spent time with family, your future in that sport was the topic of conversation. And now that anticipation of success is gone. You didn't make it. The dream is over and you grumble to yourself, *What's left to talk about now that I have failed in the thing that has defined me?*

Falling short in life. Maybe you cannot pinpoint one isolated, devastating failure like I can, but your story is a series of small decisions and circumstances that have led to where you are today—a feeling of complete defeat and failure. Life has not been kind. It has, well, *fallen short.*

Experience has taught me that failure casts a wide net. No one is immune. In fact, I am convinced that at one level or another we have all tasted the bitter fruit of failure. We have all *fallen short* at one time or another; the only variant is the degree of that failure and its subsequent consequences. And in order to come back from failure there are some key principles for you to grasp.

What makes me such an expert? My résumé is filled with

failures. In fact, I am a self-proclaimed expert on failing! Consider the following facts. I started a carpet cleaning business at age sixteen in my parents' garage, only to end up five years later accused of a multimillion dollar Wall Street fraud and secretly doing business with the New York Mafia. I was convicted of fifty-seven counts, sentenced to twenty-five years, and ordered to pay twenty-six million dollars in restitution.

I also failed as an athlete. Growing up, I dreamed of making it to the NFL or NBA. But to ensure that this athletic dream would come true I abused anabolic steroids. During my days as a high-rolling businessman, I still worked out hard and trained tenaciously. Of course, many were stronger and faster than I was, not to mention that small matter of prison. As a result of the steroid abuse, I still suffer many painful side effects, the worst of which is total sterility—resulting in my inability to have children naturally.

When I left prison in 1995 with high hopes of a stable life, I fell in love and got married. Three years later, that marriage failed. Then I tried to start a business to take advantage of the big 1990s dot-com craze, but that business failed and I was left with debt.

I accepted a job as the senior pastor of a growing church in San Diego in 1997. The staff offices and the pews were filled with incredible people. They had confidence in me and gave me the second chance I desired with all my heart. But I almost ruined the church through a series of bad decisions, and I have no one to blame but myself.

Pretty bleak . . . but that is only half of my story. This book is about the second half. I wrote it for one reason: to encourage you. No matter where you are in your life or what you have done, if you apply these steps to your life you *can* come back from failure. Sure, the degree of your comeback may vary, as all of our situations are unique, but the direction of your life will forever change by applying these steps.

If you are still not convinced that comebacks are possible, consider one of my favorite stories. It is the powerful and well-known account of Abraham Lincoln. I love the way author Michelle Magennis illustrates the comeback spirit that weaved its way through the life of our sixteenth president. She writes:

> He lost his first job as clerk in Denton Offutt's store, when Offutt's business enterprise collapsed. In 1833, Lincoln and Berry, a successor store, failed, leaving the partners in debt. Lincoln spent the next seventeen years of his life paying off the money he borrowed from friends to start his business.
>
> In 1832, in his first campaign for the state legislature, he finished eight from thirteen candidates. In a campaign document he stated that if he were to lose, he "was too familiar with disappointments to be very much chagrined." In 1835 Lincoln was engaged to be married, but his sweetheart died and his heart was broken. In 1836 he had a nervous breakdown and spent six months confined to his bed.
>
> The middle part of Abraham Lincoln's life was spent in Springfield. There he became a successful lawyer and made a brief foray into national politics. He still faced identity issues. He broke off his engagement to Mary Todd and, as a result, experienced a profound depression. However a year later he reconnected with Mary and he went on to marry her in November of 1842. Lincoln and Mary had four children.

In 1836, Lincoln won election to Congress. After his term ended, Lincoln spent the next five years focusing on his law practice. In 1854, he came back to the political arena and one of the first things he did was to oppose the Kansas-Nebraska Act, which threatened to extend slavery to other states. In 1855 Lincoln ran for the Senate but was defeated.

The next year he ran for vice President and was also defeated.

Lincoln's years of persistence and hard work eventually paid off in 1860 when he was elected as the sixteenth President of the United States of America. However, failure characterized the first two years of Lincoln's Presidency. The radicals pushed him to declare emancipation a war aim while conservatives tried to pull him away from making it a "a war about the Negro." His party suffered losses in the mid-term elections. Gradually, Lincoln grew into the President who saved America.[1]

You, too, can come back from even your most miserable defeats. This book is about coming back from failure no matter how badly you may have failed in the past. Let's start with Step One.

———

NOTE: Where personal letters and e-mails have been used in the text, they have been edited for grammar and clarity. Contact information including e-mail addresses and phone numbers, has been removed from e-mails.

Step One

IT'S ALL ABOUT YOU!

The real glory is being knocked to your knees and then coming back. That's real glory. That's the essence of it.
—VINCE LOMBARDI (1913–1970),
legendary NFL coach

"How many?" the waiter asked automatically.

"There'll be three of us," I said, "and if possible, can we have a quiet table off in a corner?" No sooner had I asked the question than I realized that it was three o'clock in the afternoon; not the restaurant's busiest time. The waiter frowned at me, as if I was rubbing it in that the place was virtually empty. But I did not have time to worry about what he thought of me. I was undercover, trying to gather information for the FBI and the SEC on what I knew was a massive, international fraud. But what I knew and what I could prove were two different things. That is the dilemma of being in the fraud-uncovering business.

"Very well, Mr. Minkow. Follow me," he mumbled and proceeded to lead me to a table near a window. Arthur's Landing overlooks the Hudson River and, although it's in New Jersey, it has a stunning view of Midtown Manhattan. I sat down, carefully unfolded my napkin, and tried to let the scenery calm my nerves.

I was worried about two things. The most obvious cause for anxiety was I was meeting with two perpetrators, Kayel Deangelis and Derek Turner. Deangelis, a young and apparently savvy New York stockbroker, knew the markets and, to my disadvantage, was also streetwise. He was the kind of guy who could see through my front if he examined me closely. My plan was to gather enough evidence on Deangelis so the FBI could pressure him into cooperating against Turner, the main player in the scheme.

If there is one thing the FBI taught me back in the 1980s when they successfully prosecuted and convicted me of fraud, it was the valuable nature of a cooperating witness who is on the inside of the scheme. I was certain Kayel Deangelis would cooperate. I just needed to gather the proof and let the FBI handle the rest.

Which brought up my second cause for concern—maintaining my cover. I didn't want the perpetrators to look too hard at the illusion I was creating. In this case, I had the luxury of being able to use my real name and position as the senior pastor of Community Bible Church in San Diego; my cover story was that I was looking to invest money from our church building fund. But there was always a chance that Turner or Deangelis would find out my affiliation with the Fraud Discovery Institute. That would tip them off that I was more than a pastor and that their scheme was probably being infiltrated. And the possibility of infiltration has every con man quaking in his loafers.

After all, there had been some recent press about how an ex-con had just uncovered a multimillion-dollar fraud, and I worried that either Kayel Deangelis or Derek Turner had read it. I tried to rationalize that with all the newspapers, cable channels, and

Internet news agencies, dilution worked in my favor. The fact that Turner was based in the Bahamas also worked to my advantage, as he would not likely receive American newspapers. At least I prayed that was the case.

I reviewed my notes for the meeting and noted what I believed was the smoking-gun evidence that Turner and Deangelis were perpetrating a fraud. I thumbed through the promised returns of 38.8 percent per year dating back to 1997. It was June of 2004 at the time of our meeting, and that meant a seven-year track record of 38.8 percent annual returns from trading index options on Wall Street! In fact, Turner had claimed to be profitable every month of those seven years. But I had done my homework and checked with Wall Street's best index option traders. They all told me the same thing: "No one could ever maintain 38.8 percent annual returns for seven years month after month with no losing months. Too many draw-down periods. Totally impossible."

I also had found an article in an obscure Australian newspaper reporting that the ASIC (Australia's version of the Securities and Exchange Commission) had shut down Turner in November of 2000—something that would make his seven years of consistent returns impossible. You cannot generate these kinds of returns while you are shut down! Moreover, this encounter with law enforcement in Australia was not disclosed in the prospectus that sat in front of me. But the worst part of this deal was the $500 million that Mr. Turner said was invested in the fund by people from all over the world—especially in the United States.

I glanced out at the city skyline, trying to identify Wall Street from across the Hudson, and thought about all the people that had placed their life savings in Turner's investments. I *had* to stop him. I had to gather the evidence for the FBI. They believed I could and because of their faith and confidence I was even more motivated to perform. I glanced at my watch. It was 3:15 p.m. I turned and looked at the front door of the restaurant. Sure enough, they were entering the room and glancing around for me.

While I took one last sip of ice water the words of my wife, Lisa, invaded my thoughts: *Barry, you're a father of twin boys now. I don't want you risking your life going undercover anymore. I don't care that the FBI has sanctioned it. You could still get hurt.* She would always end with, "I just don't understand what drives you to keep doing this undercover stuff!" But that is because my wife has never failed like I have.

———

The year was 1988 and it was Thanksgiving Day. I was living in the maximum-security unit, affectionately called "the Hole," in Terminal Island Federal Prison. The cell in which I lived was approximately five feet by seven feet. It was decorated in the latest industrial fashion: fine stainless steel (the toilet and sink) and concrete (the walls and floor). Actually, I was surrounded by steel. For example, the bunk beds were made with steel, as was the wire mesh that covered the window so no one residing in the cell could see anything out of the window, assuredly by design.

And of course, there was the cell's steel door that had a trap cut out of the middle for the purpose of passing food through to inmates. The orderlies or guards performed the perfunctory task of sliding our meal trays through the slot three times a day. But at night, even the steel trap door was shut and bolted down. Added security, I thought. Our cell also had the unique distinction of being cluttered with paperwork, transcripts, and court documents from my long, drawn-out criminal trial.

But for me, this Thanksgiving Day was memorable. My four-and-a-half-month trial was coming to an end. The government had called forty-eight witnesses to the stand, all of whom essentially said the same thing: "Barry Minkow was the mastermind of the fraud, he was in control, he knew everything that went on in the company, and the Mafia did not force him to lie to Wall Street."

My defense was to do what I did my whole life when something had gone wrong: blame someone else! I claimed that the Mafia made me lie, cheat, and steal. They forced me to live in a five-thousand-square-foot house and drive a Ferrari Testarossa! Not surprisingly, the jury didn't buy it.

My cellmate was John Hensley, a fifty-four-year-old bank robber with spider web tattoos on his elbows. We got along well, mostly because I was in trial all day and he had the cell to himself. Our dinner routine was simple and never changed.

Hensley had the bottom bunk bed and I climbed down from the top bunk to sit on his while we ate our meals together. Unfortunately for me, that meant facing the stainless steel toilet while gulping down food. How appetizing. But I was really looking forward to a good meal this Thanksgiving. The rumor was that on Thanksgiving, the food at Terminal Island was excellent. Because I was in trial every day and fed at the courthouse, my diet had consisted of baloney and cheese on white bread, two vanilla cream cookies, some stale potato chips, and juice which was so bad the inmates had a name for it: "Jim Jones Juice." Yep, I was looking forward to a good meal.

Unfortunately, the Hole was located so far away from the dining hall that when our meals were delivered in carts they first had to be reheated in microwave ovens before being distributed. The problem was that each Styrofoam tray contained meals with *all* of the courses (salad, Jell-O, turkey, and so on). I wasn't aware of that grim fact yet. I anxiously grabbed my Thanksgiving meal, sat down on Hensley's bottom bunk bed, and yanked it open. Much to my surprise, the Jell-O was runny and the salad was wilted due to the nuking process. The tiny portion of turkey was sucked dry of moisture and coagulated right before my eyes.

I angrily closed my tray and looked at Hensley who, because of his experience in prisons, had not complained and was already inhaling his meal. After glancing at Hensley, I looked at the stainless steel toilet inches from my face and at eye level, then I looked at the steel door that would not open and only had the trap part of it flipped outward to distribute the meals, then I looked at the concrete walls and quickly to the window that I could not see out of because of the steel mesh, and finally rested my eyes on the paperwork from my trial that littered the cell. I thought to myself, *Maybe it's me. Maybe when they go to all this trouble to lock someone up in such an intentional way, maybe there is something wrong with me. Maybe it isn't someone else's fault. Maybe I am where I am today on Thanksgiving Day 1988 because I am to blame.* Ouch!

It was one of the most liberating moments in all my life. I instantly had clarity. The lights flickered on and the comeback began, albeit very slowly. I was in the Hole at Terminal Island because of *me*. Rick Warren may have begun his runaway best-selling book *The Purpose Driven Life* with the phrase "it's not about you," but in coming back from failure, the first step is acknowledging the opposite—*it is* all *about you.*

———

In today's society, we have become masters at avoiding unpleasant or harsh terminology. For example, companies do not talk about people getting fired anymore because *getting fired* sounds so negative. Instead they use terms like *rightsizing* or *downsizing*. Car dealers have also succumbed to this methodology. Instead of selling used cars, they now sell preowned cars. I guess it takes the sting out of buying a car that isn't new. In fact, you can even get a *certified* pre-owned car. Now, in case you are suspicious that it had not really been pre-owned and that the dealer may be trying to pawn off one of those new cars on you, it is certified pre-owned! According to author and pastor John Ortberg, even shoplifters have different names now. They are no longer referred to as shoplifters but *cost of living adjustment specialists*. In truth, that term could potentially apply to just about everyone!

Now contrast the above examples with a true story from seventeenth-century England. Lord Protector Oliver Cromwell was posing for a portrait and became increasingly frustrated with the artist's inability to paint reality. He stopped long enough to stare deep into the eyes of the artist and then said, "Listen to me, when you paint me you paint me warts and all."

But in my life I discovered I did whatever I could to avoid having people see the real Barry Minkow. Not only was I concealing my fraud, I was also hiding the person behind the fraud. Why? I cared so much about what others thought of me that I wanted to control everyone's impression of me. Particularly when I failed. And I did this in every area of my life.

If I was late for a meeting, it was not because I was irresponsible; it was a traffic problem. If sales were down, it was not because I was lazy and not adequately following up leads, but market conditions. I so desired to control people's impression of me that I was self-deceived. Self-deception is the greatest obstacle to rebounding from failure. Why? Because if the problem is anything but *me*, then I will never go through the other nine steps that will help me come back from failure. When the blame for failure can be laid at someone else's doorstep, learning my culpability in the failure is no longer relevant.

That is why if you are going to come back from failure, there must come a point in time when the self-deception stops; a time when you resist the temptation to try to control people's impression of you and lay it on the line. A time when you say, "Maybe it's me. Maybe it is not market conditions, the fact that I was not breast-fed as a kid, my ex-wife or ex-husband, my parents, my children, my former business partner, or any other external factors. Maybe I am where I am at today because of me!" It will be your very own Thanksgiving Day experience, minus the cell. But when coming back from failure, the first step is acknowledging that it is all about you.

So what does this step look like? I don't know because I do not know your unique situation. However, I do know what it *does not* look like. For example, if, in explaining a past or present failure in your life, you use qualifying phrases like: "The business failed *but* . . ." or "I did not make the team *because* . . ." or "My marriage failed *due to* . . ." or "I am in prison *on account of* . . ."

you should take a close look at what you're saying. You can fill in the blanks because we have all, in an effort to control people's impression of us, used these qualifying phrases in an effort to explain away failure.

My advice? Try this: "My business failed" (period). "My marriage failed" (period). "I did not make the team" (period). "I am going to prison" (period). "I made serious mistakes as a parent" (period). When you are able to drop the qualifiers while telling your story, you have met and satisfied the requirement of the first step to rebounding from failure. Become comfortable using the first-person point of view, because step one is all about you.

And do you know what's ironic about step one? The very people you sought to hide from so desperately by using qualifiers to explain failure will be far more impressed with your humility and ownership of the failure then they ever would have been when you attempted to justify it. People will forgive you. In fact, they will be more willing to *give* you a second chance when you have volitionally chosen ownership of past failures instead of playing the qualifying blame game. As Oliver Cromwell would say, "Tell your story, warts and all."

Experience has taught me that because people are forgiving and receptive to genuine ownership of failure, it is highly likely that someone will give you another chance. For a convicted felon, that person is the one who provides the first job upon release. For the entrepreneur, it is the investor who says, "You have learned from your past failures and I am going to give you another shot." For the divorced, it is that special person who decides to assume the best about your potential and not dwell on your past . . . and says yes to the proposal.

I have much to say about these special "paramedic" type of people later in the book, but for now it should be noted that for convicted felons the first person to typically believe in us is our criminal lawyer, and in my case that was the very competent David Kenner. The second person who believed in me was far less predictable. In fact, he was the last person in the world I would have ever expected to risk taking a chance on Barry Minkow.

———

Within weeks of my release after serving eighty-seven months in federal prison, Dave Nezbit, the very FBI agent who supervised my investigation during the ZZZZ Best fraud, asked me to spend a week in Quantico, Virginia, training FBI agents on the techniques perpetrators use to deceive their victims. He explained that I would have to spend a week at the facility sleeping in the dorms with the agents in training. Since 11 September 2001, the FBI no longer allows nonagents to spend the night at their facilities. But in May of 1995, I was allowed. And there I was: one month sleeping in a federal prison and the next month spending a week at FBI training headquarters teaching agents.

Because Nezbit gave me this opportunity, it suddenly became OK for other organizations to invite me to speak at their events. It was like the FBI had imputed credibility to me, and others followed suit. Dave Nezbit's words to me upon my release are still fresh in my mind: "Barry, I've heard you turned your life around in prison. I believe everyone deserves a second chance—*especially those who accept responsibility for their failures.*"

The last person or organization in the world that I had expected to give me a second chance was the FBI! But they did, and therefore an incredible loyalty was established that exists to this day. They were the first nonfamily members to believe in me. It is for this reason that I always tell employers who are looking for good people to look for those who *have* failed in the past. When given the opportunity to prove themselves, two things will inevitably happen.

First, they will work harder than anyone else, since they realize they are not starting from "neutral." They have something to prove or overcome, and their work ethic will often reflect that fact. Secondly, more often than not they will be the most loyal employees simply because they were given a chance. And for those of us who have failed and accepted the "it's all about me" reality of that failure, a second chance is all we could ever ask for.

My wife, Lisa, understands that now, but she didn't back when I was at Arthur's Landing sitting at a table overlooking Midtown Manhattan and awaiting the perpetrators behind a multimillion-dollar international fraud. In my mind, I owed the FBI. They had believed in me ten years earlier when I was first released from prison, and I was determined not to let them down. I was going to get the evidence they needed to shut down this fraud, no matter what! And I did.

———

"It's a real honor to meet you, Mr. Turner. Kayel has told me so much about you," I stated as we sat down after the customary handshakes and introductions. Derek Turner looked to be in his late forties and was a squinting version of Dennis Hopper. He'd been told I was the senior pastor of a large church in San Diego and that we wanted to place the two million dollars that had accumulated in our building fund into an investment opportunity that would provide returns in excess of the 2.5 percent our bank savings account was offering at the time.

To convince Turner that I was really a qualified investor, I had Kayel Deangelis fly out to San Diego and observe one of our weekend services. When he attended the church, the pews were packed and we had just completed renovations, spending close to two million dollars in the process. Deangelis reported back to Turner that the church was "the real deal" and most certainly had the two million to invest with Turner's firm, Turning International.

To further ensure my success as a potential investor, the FBI created a bank statement for the church that showed we had over two million dollars in our checking account. In my experience as a former perpetrator, the best time to gather information from potential fraudulent schemers is when they are convinced you have big money to invest. If the investment deal is truly a fraud, the perpetrators have a heightened sense of urgency to raise money to pay off investors who came into the deal at the beginning. Keeping everyone happy is the key to pulling off a scam, and that means the constant pressure of raising new capital. I knew that pressure only too well.

Turner was claiming that Turning International had over $500 million under management. The fact that my measly two million dollar investment, which represented less than 1 percent of the total fund, was able to persuade him to fly from the Bahamas (where Turning International was located) to New York to meet with me personally was certainly a red flag. Someone who actually did have $500 million under management and who was able to generate 38.5 percent annual returns wouldn't be that motivated by my business! Just do the math—at 38.8 percent annually with $500 million under management, it would take less than a week to earn two million dollars.

Derek Turner pulled out three thick volumes of charts that he spread out over two tables at the restaurant. These were charts that documented market fluctuations going back to 1997. They contained dates and lines and ratios and numbers—most of which made no sense to me. Turner spent an hour explaining that whether the market went up or down, he would be there to make a profit. Kayel Deangelis added that his father had over one million dollars in the Turner fund and was extremely happy. I made a mental note of that fact. Deangelis was helping Turner sell the fund, but he actually believed that Turner was generating these 38.8 percent annual returns. He truly believed in Turner, but as a streetwise broker, he should have known better.

After his chart presentation I asked only one question. It was the question that would confirm to the FBI, the SEC, and me whether or not Turner was legit. It was also the one question I could not answer when I was perpetrating the ZZZZ Best fraud. That question is: What is the independent proof of profitability? Anyone who has ever been a con artist must deal with it and that's exactly where the evidence lies. Because Turner had already said he did not have audited financial statements from a certified public accounting firm, I did not ask for financial statements. Instead I simply asked for trading records; records that would corroborate from the brokerage firm he was dealing with that Turning International actually generated the returns he was claiming with a source independent of him.

"No one sees my trading records, Mr. Minkow. Period, end of discussion," Turner growled. In an instant I knew he was a fraud. Whenever a wall is erected between the investor and due diligence it is a red flag for fraud. For example, in the ZZZZ Best fraud case, the auditors asked to see the restoration jobs I was allegedly performing which accounted for 86 percent of our revenue. My standard story to investors was that we would repair buildings damaged by water or fire by extracting the water damage, deodorizing and sanitizing all affected areas, and removing and repairing flooring where necessary.

Accountants and investors pushed me for specific addresses, but I refused to provide them, citing confidentiality. However, the real reason I did not provide addresses was simple—the jobs did not exist. In like manner, Turner was not doing any trading (or if he was, it was not profitable) or he would have gladly shared the proof of that success, especially if it increased his ability to raise money.

I left the meeting and reported to the FBI everything that happened. Special Agent Matt Galioto was in charge of the case. After the Arthur's Landing meeting, Matt asked if I would be willing to go to a series of meetings with Turner and his associates where I would wear a wire. I agreed. The first meeting would be with Kayel Deangelis, where our hopes were that he would say enough incriminating things that the FBI could later persuade him to cooperate. I met with him at the Sheraton Hotel in Hartford, Connecticut, and wore the wire.

The meeting went well, and days later Matt Galioto paid a surprise visit to Deangelis, who by then had opened a Turning International office in Melville Long Island, and explained that the FBI had enough evidence to prosecute him but would not if he helped gather evidence on Turner. He agreed and began taping calls whenever Turner called from the Bahamas. I actually felt bad for Deangelis because of his father's one million dollar investment in Turner's venture.

To secure evidence against Turner, Matt Galioto regularly listened in on our phone conversations and recorded them for the purpose of preserving Turner's multiple misrepresentations about the fund's size and expected investor returns. As a prospective investor, these taped phone calls corroborated what Turner typically promised potential investors in order to persuade them to invest.

However, when Matt visited the US Attorney in Long Island to present the case for prosecution, the Assistant US Attorney said there was still something missing. He wanted to make sure that Mr. Turner was lying to investors to get them into the fund. There were two ways to prove that. First, I had to try to obtain the trading records. This would be difficult to secure because Turner could conceivably be trading at many brokerage firms; far too many to nail down.

The second way to prove he was lying was to show he didn't have $500 million in deposits, a statement prominently plastered all over his investor materials. The government's smoking-gun evidence in investment fraud cases is always the material that the investor relied upon to make the decision to invest. If the investor relied on facts about the company that were not true, the playing field was not level and that constitutes material fraud. And fraud, as I'd found out the hard way twenty years earlier, is the government's most actionable of all white-collar crimes.

We knew from Turner's wiring instructions to investors that he banked at Scotia Bank in the Bahamas and Matt Galioto had, by calling in a number of favors, subpoenaed those bank statements. They confirmed that Turner had only about a million dollars. That Matt Galioto was able to get these bank statements was the key to proving fraud in the case. Why? If Scotia Bank was the only bank Derek Turner was using, he was 499 million dollars short—and therefore lying to investors about his true financial condition.

Matt Galioto and the US Attorney in New York asked me to fly along with two FBI agents to the Bahamas, wear a wire, and see if Derek Turner would confirm that he "only banks at Scotia bank and there are no other bank accounts for Turning International." The trip was complicated by the fact that the two FBI agents were not allowed to carry guns in a foreign country, so there was an increased risk for me.

———

"I need to do this, Lisa," I explained while looking straight into her clear blue eyes. "I need to travel to the Bahamas and get this evidence for the FBI and shut this guy down." We were at home trying to carry on the conversation while our eighteen-month-old twin boys were treating us like human jungle gyms.

"Why do you need to do this?" she pleaded. It was the first time I'd actually told her. Up until that point she had thought I was motivated by the guilt of my past frauds. I gently put the boys down on the carpet.

"Because the FBI gave me a second chance when it was not the popular thing to do. I feel obligated. I feel it is the right thing to do." I paused, allowing the words to sink in. "You have never failed. You do not know what it is like to walk by people who smirk as they recognize you but say nothing. You do not know what it is like to fail publicly and be totally abandoned. You don't know how it is to have people always assume the worst about you. And you do not know what it is like to be told 'once a con man, always a con man.' But I do. People hold my past against me all the time. That's just the way it is. But the FBI gave me a chance and ten years later they are not sorry for it." I paused briefly. She was listening attentively.

"Do you know why they gave me another chance? Because I proclaimed to everyone who would listen for almost eight years in prison that *I* was the reason ZZZZ Best failed and I had finally stopped blaming others for my mistakes. And that's why they gave me a second chance. And because they believed in me, I want to do great things for them . . . no matter what the cost. I have to do this, Lisa," I said with conviction.

As she contemplated my words, she stood up, walked over to the dresser and turned to face me. "I always believed in you," she said. "And I still do." I silently applauded her, sprang from the floor, and gave her a big hug. The boys watched momentarily, before settling back in to play.

"Go shut this guy down," she instructed. I was happy to comply.

———

During the trip to the Bahamas I met with Derek Turner in person twice. "Our church is ready to invest the two million dollars," I promised. "The church only has one requirement. Because you are not in the United States, they want to know what happens to our money once it hits Scotia Bank. Do you send it off to Switzerland or some other country or to another bank in the Bahamas?"

Without hesitation Mr. Turner said, "The only accounts we have for Turning International are with Scotia Bank. There are no other banks in this country or in Switzerland. Scotia Bank is our only bank and always will be our only bank."

Bingo. I got him! On the plane ride home I thought about Dave Nezbit, who was now long retired from the FBI. I wondered if he knew how much he had impacted my life by giving me a chance to prove myself. I didn't know the answer to that question. But the one thing I did know is that unless I'd begun with accepting responsibility for what I did and truly believed that my failure was *all about me*, he never would have given me that chance. That much I knew for certain. The same will ring true for you, because the first step to coming back from failure is realizing that it truly is *all about you.*

ROBERT E. KESSLER
STAFF WRITER, *Newsday*

April 20, 2005

Ex-con man stars in sting. Former stock swindler Barry Minkow, now a minister, helps the FBI in the arrest of a man on LI who allegedly ran a phony hedge fund scheme.

A pastor writing sermons by day. An undercover investigator at night.

That's how Barry Minkow, a former notorious stock swindler, describes his life since he got out of federal prison nearly 10 years ago.

His most recent undercover work for the FBI led earlier this week to the arrest in Melville of a man who allegedly was running a phony hedge fund, said Minkow, an evangelical minister in San Diego who also has set up a business to help track down stock swindlers.

Calling himself "a liar and thief spared by the grace of God," Minkow has been credited by the FBI and other law enforcement agencies with helping them catch a number of swindlers, including confidence men in California and Chicago who were targeting members of churches, U.S. Marines, and athletes.

"People can ask for forgiveness and find all that contentment . . . that I couldn't find with my 5,000-square-foot house, Ferrari, and money," Minkow said. "I've been out of prison for 10 years, and I have found that contentment."

In the 1980s, Minkow masterminded the $300-million ZZZZ Best fraud, for which he was sent to prison for seven years. Minkow started his endeavor in his mother's garage in Reseda, Calif., when he was 16 years old.

The business revolved around a supposed carpet-cleaning firm that federal prosecutors showed actually was a Ponzi scheme, a scam in which investors are paid returns from money raised from subsequent investors, rather than from profits generated by a real business.

Minkow said he was stealing from relatives, including his grandmother, to support the scam and also managed to keep ZZZZ Best going by borrowing money from organized crime figures in Queens at extortionate rates of 250 percent a year.

In a telephone interview from his San Diego office, Minkow said that whoever else might have lost money in his scheme, he made sure he repaid the mob figures first.

In the interview and in two recent autobiographies, *Cleaning Up* and *Clean Sweep*, Minkow said he was raised as a Jew but became a born-again Christian through the inspiration of a Christian counselor before he entered prison, and then through a cellmate.

The man arrested on Long Island through Minkow's work, Derek Turner, a New Zealand native, was arraigned Monday by Magistrate James Orenstein at the U.S. District Court in Central Islip.

At a bail hearing Thursday, Turner's attorney Joseph Conway, of the Mineola firm of LaRusso and Conway, said he was still in the process of gathering bail for his client. Conway, the former head of the U.S. attorney's office on Long Island, previously has said that his client, who operated Turning International, Ltd. from the Bahamas and a branch office in Melville, is innocent.

Assistant U.S. Attorney Mark Lesko, considering Turner's actions, said that he was "a considerable flight risk."

Minkow said he got involved in the Long Island case when a lawyer for his San Diego business, the Fraud Discovery Institute, told him about a client who had been solicited by Turner's fund.

After several months of taping meetings and telephone

conversations, Minkow was invited to meet with Turner in the Bahamas, where he secretly recorded what court documents say were incriminating conversations.

Some have questioned Minkow's motives for his current persona, contending that his dual roles as pastor and undercover investigator might be some type of new scam.

In prison, he said, some fellow inmates taunted him by saying he would be "born again till you're out again."

But Minkow said he should be judged on the good he has done through his Fraud Discovery Institute.

He said his best reference is the federal judge who originally denied him a lenient sentence after he was convicted in the ZZZZ Best case.

Two years ago, the judge, impressed by Minkow's work, released him from probation three years early, saying, "We have another problem facing our country now with corporate dishonesty. . . . Go in and investigate some of these frauds, as [the federal prosecutor in your case now] says that you're doing, and bring others to justice."[1]

Step Two

DON'T FAIL FAILURE

"Success consists of going from failure to failure without loss of enthusiasm."

—WINSTON CHURCHILL (1874-1965),
Prime Minister of the UK

Mr. Minkow . . . *Mr. Minkow!"*
I glanced up quickly at the person demanding my attention. I had drifted off, reminiscing about how much Room 106 of the Dirksen Senate Office building in Washington DC resembled the federal courthouse in Los Angeles where I had been convicted after a prolonged four-and-a-half-month criminal trial back in 1988. Each one of the rooms possessed the intimidating backdrop of the legal power of the United States government built solidly into the architecture. Ornate and official looking seals were delicately carved into the polished wood walls.

Moreover, ranking committee member Senator Herb Kohl possessed an eerie resemblance to Judge Dickran Tevrizian, the federal judge who had presided over my trial. The points of similarity between my memories and the present caused my palms to sweat and anxiety to settle in firmly. Senator Kohl and Judge Tevrizian both spoke from elevated platforms, which meant they looked down on me no matter if I was sitting or standing. And if that was not enough, even the stenographers looked alike! It never ceases to amaze me what details the human brain chooses to remember in times of great stress.

As was the case in my criminal trial, people I did not know, mostly media, were compressed in the seats of the room with their notepads ready to capture the day's events. Only a wooden gate separated the audience from those who were testifying. And just as I had worried years before what would be written about me, I once again was concerned about what these reporters would write about my Senate testimony.

I surveyed the room one more time, wiped my sweaty palms on my freshly creased suit pants, and grabbed a swig from the water bottle in front of me. *Why did I agree to do this?* I thought to myself.

Only two of us were testifying that morning. Ruth Mitchell, a pleasant elderly lady from Pittsburgh, Pennsylvania, was planted on my right. Ruth and her husband, Len, had lost a hundred thousand dollars in an investment that was brought to them by their CPA—a man named Barry Korcan. Korcan owned a large CPA firm in Beaver, Pennsylvania. She explained that he first befriended her, and then swindled 11.5 million dollars from her and thirty-nine other victims over a ten-year period.

She added that Korcan and his wife, Heidi, lived an extravagant lifestyle that included the purchase of new Cadillacs, boats, sports cars, vacations, homes, and the like. I felt like interrupting her and saying, "What did you expect? We who perpetrate fraud do not steal money to save it, but rather we steal money to spend it." But I decided to keep my comments to myself. The last thing

I needed at that moment was a swift blow to the head with an elderly lady's pocketbook!

However, no matter how badly Mrs. Mitchell portrayed Barry Korcan, the CPA who ended up pleading guilty to the crime, I could not get angry with him. Not because I did not think his crime was particularly evil, because it was. It dealt a financial blow to elderly victims that they will probably never fully recover from. Instead, it was because I knew one thing that Mrs. Mitchell, Senator Kohl, and the media listening attentively that morning did not know about Barry Korcan.

Simply stated, no one goes to school for years to earn his or her CPA license with the intent of ending up in prison for an $11 million fraud. Something happened in his life that triggered the downward spiral that led to his fraud conviction. All of us who have failed share that common experience. I strayed down the same path many years ago.

SCOTCHGARD

I was fourteen years old. My mom worked at a carpet cleaning company, Same Day Carpet Care in Mission Hills, California, and in her position as office manager, she was able to get me work as a carpet cleaner's helper during the summer months and on weekends. I would go out as an apprentice on residential carpet cleaning jobs. For a fourteen-year-old, this was an awesome responsibility.

My job as a helper was to keep my mouth shut and move furniture, "push the wand"—which meant doing the actual carpet cleaning—and filling and emptying water buckets. On this particular day, it was a bright and shiny summer Saturday morning in August. My crew leader, Joel, and I polished off our morning donuts and coffee and headed to the first customer's home located not far from the office.

We were scheduled to clean a living room, dining room, hallway, and three bedrooms for the price of $69.95. It was an easy job, so I had most of the work done within two hours. As we were leaving, the customer asked Joel the key question, "How can I keep my carpets looking *this clean*?" I had come to learn that while carpet was wet it looked clean, but when it dried stubborn spots would reappear. Thus, the opportunity to sell the customer additional products was that tight window between wet and dry carpeting.

Her question was Joel's cue to launch into his standard sales presentation. I had heard him give it a million times and could repeat it verbatim if asked. But I was a young teenager and my job was to be quiet and do the work. "Your day to sell will come when you are older," Joel would always say with a wink.

"Well, ma'am," he began, "I would recommend that you apply Scotchgard on the carpets to protect them from resoiling." She paused and contemplated his suggestion. Her silence was an additional invitation to persuade.

"You see, ma'am," Joel stated factually, "your third largest investment next to your house and then your car is your carpeting! And if you wanted to replace your carpeting it would be quite expensive. So that is why I recommend Scotchgard, which acts like a liquid plastic protecting your carpets from resoiling and wear and tear." No matter how many times I had heard it, I remember thinking what a great line that was . . . "Your third largest investment next to your house and your car is your carpets."

She tilted her head to the side, raised her brows and asked, "How much extra would that cost?" At this point I knew he had her. Whenever the customer asked the "how much" question, they were already essentially committing to the purchase. The only detail that remained was agreeing on a price. So Joel pulled out his tape measure and began to walk around the home measuring this and that—stopping only to record a certain measurement. I stood there awkwardly, trying to make frivolous conversation with the lady. Joel then did some simple calculations before he finally blurted out the cost.

"One hundred dollars."

He really could have said any number at this point but a hundred bucks for two guys on the commission of 40 percent of what we brought in was enough. The customer thought about it for a moment, contemplated the cost of replacement, and then looked down to the fresh, clean smelling carpets. "OK," she nodded in agreement. "Go ahead."

At this point, I had reached the end of my ability to casually converse with an adult. I excused myself and immediately darted out to our truck while Joel prepared the contract. My normal routine in these instances was to fill up a Hudson sprayer with Scotchgard, spray it on the carpeting while it was still wet, and then rake it in with a carpet rake. Only this time, to my utter shock, I realized as I searched the back of the truck frantically that I had forgotten to load the gallon of Scotchgard!

I did not know what to do. I was afraid to go into the house and tell Joel that I forgot the Scotchgard and as a result we would lose a one-hundred-dollar sale. I decided to be mature about the situation. So I sat in the cabin of the truck and cried. I knew fourteen years old was too young to be an apprentice and Joel was kind enough, with the addition of motherly persuasion, to hire me. Now I had blown a sale. I just knew that Joel would look me square in the eye and shout, "You're fired!"

It only took about ten minutes before Joel sensed that something was wrong. He marched up to the truck but paused when he saw me crying through the window.

"What's the matter? Why aren't you applying the Scotchgard?" he asked.

"Because . . . I forgot . . . to load it this morning . . . at the office," I said between snivels, "And now we are going to lose a one-hundred-dollar sale!"

Joel glanced at me with a reassuring grin. "No we're not," he whispered as he leaned into the truck. "Just spray water—she'll never know the difference."

I was glued to my seat in disbelief as he rounded the truck, pulled the Hudson sprayer from the back and added a little bubble gum deodorizer (to make it appear that it wasn't just water). He strode straight through the lawn, unrolled the garden hose, and filled up the sprayer. I had exited the truck to watch him, and by this time I knew that he wasn't kidding.

"Go apply it," he ordered. And I did. The homeowner hovered behind me in the living room as I sprayed the Scotchgard and exclaimed, "Boy, that Scotchgard sure smells good." I turned to smile at her halfheartedly but could not bring myself to look her in the eye.

We finished the job and went back to the office. I anxiously waited for the phone to ring. I just knew that the customer would call and say, "I had my carpet fibers analyzed and I know you sprayed water and not Scotchgard and you're a big fraud!"

But much to my surprise that Saturday afternoon, there was no such call. So I slept restlessly that night and knew that the call would surely come Monday morning. But Monday also came and went without a call from the customer. Then the entire week passed—no call. When no call ever came I learned something that would eventually culminate in the receipt of a twenty-five-year prison sentence. I learned that the consequences for certain deceitful behaviors do not always immediately follow the actual dishonest act. Therefore, it subconsciously reinforced the behavior.

Two years later (at age sixteen), in October of 1982, I started ZZZZ Best Carpet Cleaning out of my parents' garage. Unfortunately for me, I had already learned that when faced with an obstacle or problem in a business setting, deceit worked. And I would not hesitate to exercise it as an option when the opportunity presented itself.

THE PRINCIPLE OF THE PATH

The scope of understanding that you are not alone is not limited to the fact that you and many others like you may have experienced failure of one kind or another. It's also important to identify the cause-and-effect relationship that initiated the downward regression that led to that failure in hopes of not repeating that behavior in the future. I call it "not failing failure." By unpacking and identifying the anatomy of events that led to failing, you can avoid repeating the same mistakes. And in so doing, you will realize that none of us who have failed are alone in how we got there!

About two weeks after my testimony in front of the US Senate, I was surprised to log onto my e-mail and see the following from Barry Korcan. He wrote:

———Original Message———
From: Barry Korcan
Sent: Tuesday, April 11, 2006 8:58 AM
To: info@frauddiscovery.net
Subject: RE: PLEASE READ . . . I HAVE SOME
        QUESTIONS FOR YOU.

Dear Rev. Minkow:

I saw your name in an AP news story about your testimony before the Senate on Aging. You testified with a woman named Ruth Mitchell. I am the same Barry Korcan that defrauded Len and Ruth Mitchell of their investment. I have read your Web page and feel as though God put it in my heart to contact you. I am very impressed with your accomplishments since your time in prison. Even though Ruth Mitchell believes it was an IRS audit that caught me (and it did play a part, I won't deny that), I turned myself in to the US Attorney's office in Pittsburgh before they knew anything of Guardian Investments or my illegal activities. So many things have happened to me since I decided to turn myself in, including the sudden death of my mother, recent congestive heart failure for my father, and I could go on. I

could relate the different times that I feel God has set me on
His path (emphasis mine).

I was raised Roman Catholic but in June joined the
Christian Assembly Church in Industry, PA, (www.
christianassemblychurch.org) gave my testimony before our
church on July 17th to let everyone know *who I am and how
mistakes in life can lead you down the wrong path* (emphasis
mine).

My sentencing for my crimes will take place on April
28th. I am deeply sorrowful for my crimes against the victims, the difficulty for my wife and family, and most of all
the sins against God, whom I know has already forgiven me.
I have some questions I thought you might be able to help
me with regarding your divinity degree, prison, and how you
started on your path to help people (emphasis mine).

I was wondering if you would be willing to talk with me
by e-mail or telephone. I pray you will answer my questions.

May God Bless You in Your Ministry.
Barry Korcan

Please do not miss the part in his e-mail that links together all of
us who have failed. If you read too quickly, you may have innocently passed it over and missed the most important cause-and-
effect relationship that is the common denominator with all of
us who have failed. Did you notice how many times he used the
word *path?*

Korcan uses the word *path* three times in the context of direction. And although he probably did not realize it at the time, he

hit the proverbial nail on the head. The cause-and-effect relationship of failure is called the Principle of the Path and it works like this: *Directions, not dreams, determine destinations.*[1]

Do not lose the impact of this statement in its simplicity. Go to MapQuest or Yahoo Maps and you will note that by taking a certain road you will always end up in a predictable location. That is because whatever path you choose, you automatically choose a destination with it.

Insert a starting and ending address into one of these sites. What happens next? Before you know it, you will have a map, along with detailed directions that will provide the roads necessary to get you from where you are to your intended destination. The Principle of the Path does not concern itself with things like "feelings," "motives," or "intentions." It does not work that way. The Principle of the Path means that your destination is solely determined by which direction you choose.

Right now there are approximately 2.4 million people in state or federal prisons in this country. As a veteran of several of these facilities, I learned that all 2.4 million prisoners and I share one thing in common—none of us ever planned on ending up there!

You see, my intentions when I started my company at age sixteen were not to end up in prison, but the Principle of the Path does not care about my original motives or my intentions. The moment I set my feet on the road of compromise, in both big and small ways, it had a predetermined destination: ruin! It was only a matter of time. As I would later find out in follow-up conversations with Barry Korcan, the moment he opened his own CPA practice in August of 1992 was not the start of his demise. But he can pinpoint the moment his direction shifted. It was when, as he says, some tax clients asked him to help "reduce their tax liability by hiding some income."

Once he decided to comply with the request, his days were numbered. He had set his feet on the path of compromise. The destination may not be reached tomorrow, or even next year, but it eventually leads to devastation—every time. We who have failed avoid failing failure when we learn this crucial principle.

Debt is another well-traveled path. Zero percent financing (notwithstanding common sense) tells us that once we place our feet on the road of irresponsible spending it is only a matter of time before that road leads to economic ruin and bankruptcy. So why do we do it? Why did the bankruptcy laws have to be changed in 2005 as the result of so many people filing? The answer from my own experience is: because I am smarter, more manipulative and more resourceful, and I can control outcomes. Sure, most people end up in bankruptcy racking up debt, but I am not most people. I have this big deal coming or this big sale closing and it will be taken care of. Sound familiar?

The workaholic path is also just as crowded and is certainly not limited to either sex. People come to me for counseling in my role as a pastor and this is often a common topic of strife in families. Let me first state for the record that compassion is not one of my gifts. In a typical session, the wife will look at me and groan, "My husband works thirteen hours a day and is so preoccupied with work that when he is home he is absent when he is present!" They both look at me quizzically when I respond.

"You don't need a counselor, you need to be congratulated," I say to the husband. "You would be better served with a map because your problem is geographical, not one that can be resolved in counseling," I add. (I told you I did not have the gift to be a compassionate counselor!)

I explain further in response to the startled faces and nod my head. "Yes, *congratulated* because you set your feet on the path of 'workaholism.' Thousands of people before you have done the same and this path always ends up in a predetermined destination—the destruction of a marriage. So you have *arrived* at the destination that you placed your feet on when you chose to work thirteen-hour days, six days a week."

Inevitably the husband will almost always say, "Yes, but that was not my *intention.* This is how I have to work to support my family!"

And I believe him, because when I started ZZZZ Best I also had pure intentions. The problem is the Principle of the Path does not concern itself with subjective intentions or excuses. The reality of the Principle of the Path is you place your feet on a certain path and it is only a matter of time before you arrive. It is purely objective.

The Principle of the Path also has no respect for age. How many times have I heard about the parents who beg their teenagers to realize that they might be underestimating the influence others have on their lives? So parents implore their children to make good decisions regarding their friends, because whom you hang around with in life is directly linked to how you are going to do in life. But despite the pleas, how many times has a good, loving child made some bad choices with the wrong crowd and lived to regret it? Too often. Why? Because the moment a young person places his or her feet on the path of close relationships with negative influences, it is only a matter of time before that path ends up in poor grades, drug and alcohol abuse, and sometimes even death. That's because whenever we choose a path, we automatically chose a predetermined destination with that path. It's only a matter of time.

But despite all the evidence from experience that can be dredged up, here is the sum of my experience from the perspective of serving many years in prison, ten years pastoring a church, and several years of working with law enforcement to detect fraud crimes. This experience, in addition to interacting directly with the perpetrators of those crimes, tells me about how people respond to the Principle of the Path.

- "The Principle of the Path is true—just not for me."

- "I realize that *most* CEOs that inflate earnings and hide debt end up in disgrace on the front page of the *Wall Street Journal*—but that will not happen to me."

- "I realize that *most* people who decide to cheat on final examinations get caught and the behavior becomes habit forming—but that will not happen in my case."

- "I realize that *most* people who do drugs become addicted, but not me . . . *it will never happen to me. Besides, I've got a prescription.*"

- "I realize that most people who allow the flirtation to progress to infatuation should worry, but I can still control the relationship and keep his spouse and mine in the dark."

Delusional? Hardly. People who express these views do so with a clear conscience and a steady voice. If you were to ask them how they planned on avoiding the Principle of the Path, here's what they'd say:

- "I can control outcomes."

- "I am smarter than that."

- "I have an MBA."

- "My friend so-and-so did it, and he's just fine!"

- "Yes, I acknowledge that in many cases people who place their feet on the path of compromise end up in ruin—but that's everyone else. I am very manipulative and an expert at controlling outcomes, and therefore, that will never happen to me."

These responses come despite clear evidence that millions of people before them have placed their feet on the similar path of compromise in some area of their life and ended up in ruin, yet that does not seem to be a deterrent.

THE PROBLEM

Why are so many overwhelming precedents overlooked? *Because people confuse where they are now with where they are going.* But the issue is never where you are now—it's where the path you have placed your feet on will end up. It is this notion that we can some-how control outcomes that permits us to place our feet on the path of debt and anticipate a different outcome from the scores of people who have taken that path before, only to end up in financial ruin.

Motives are not relevant, nor are good intentions. The Principle of the Path does not concern itself with those things. (I used to justify lying to banks because the use of proceeds from fraudulently obtained loans was going to my payroll to pay employees who needed to feed their families.) The culmination of my own failures has led me to understand that the Principle of the Path does not concern itself with where you are *now*—it's the direction *in which you are headed* that matters.

If there is still doubt about the validity of the Principle of the Path, please consider the following illustration. Chances are (especially if you are like me) that there is a direct correlation between where you are now and a path you have previously chosen. That is, if you are not satisfied with your life and you are in your twenties, thirties, forties, fifties, or sixties, you may be thinking, *I had this great dream and picture of how my life would turn out, but what I am experiencing today is not what I dreamed for myself years ago.* Here's the obvious question. What happened?

It could be that you have chosen a path that has led right to where you are now. Why didn't it lead somewhere different? Because the Principle of the Path cares little for our dreams and goals, it merely follows the law of geography and takes us to the ultimate destination of where we have placed our feet.

The first step to coming back from failure is the acknowledgment of the proper pronoun: *I* failed because of *me* or, again, *it is all about me.* Comeback from failure cannot begin until ownership occurs. In step two we avoid failing failure by realizing that all of our stories reveal a common denominator that links failure to a series of events that began when we placed our feet on a certain path—even though the consequences of that first step do not immediately follow the action. Our dreams and ambitions may have aspired otherwise, but what life experience proves is that paths carry with them a predetermined destination. As one of my college professors used to always say, "Life is a difficult teacher; it gives you the test first and then the lesson afterward."

But the good news is, you may be down, but you're not out! Keep reading to see how I can say that with 100 percent certainty.

I never mentioned the reason *why* I was testifying in front of the US Senate. I mean, it is not every day that a convicted felon gets that kind of an opportunity. I ask your forgiveness in advance if the letter below from seventy-nine-year-old Don Scott, addressed to Senator Herb Kohl, appears self-serving. I have included it not to impute credibility to my comeback story but to establish the truth of the matter by illustrating that once the Principle of the Path is learned and applied, coming back from failure will be the inevitable result. Count on it.

March 18th, 2006
Senator Herb Kohl
Ranking Manager
Special Committee on the Aging
Washington, DC 20510-6400

Dear Senator Kohl and Committee Members:
My name is Don Scott and I am 79 years old and I live

in Seqium, Washington. I am writing this letter in hopes that you will read it carefully and use my experiences to help others who may be what I call elderly and vulnerable.

I am a firm believer in things happening for a reason. Although my wife Judy and I live in Sequim, last January 2005 we were visiting San Diego, California. While watching the morning news on the local KUSI affiliate, I saw an interview with Barry Minkow. He was talking about his recently released book, his past life as a criminal, and his current life working undercover for law enforcement identifying financial crimes in progress. And that is when I first heard Barry mention a factoring fraud that he had uncovered totaling over 55 million dollars called MX Factors.

You see, my wife and I had recently invested $210,000 in a company called Par Three Financial. This company offered returns of 30% a year and claimed to be factoring receivables for check cashing companies. Since a banker friend of mine recommended me to the deal, I initially had no fears that the company was a solid investment. That is until I saw Barry in this interview.

Since this money was most of our life savings and since there was no possible way I could earn it again at my age, I visited Barry's church in San Diego. After a service, I introduced myself to him and explained my investment in Par Three Financial. I also gave him all the paperwork and the company web site. Barry promised that he would check it out and then he said something that I will never forget. He told me that no matter what, he would get my money back.

I felt comforted and my wife and I decided to trust Barry with what amounted to our life savings.

Within 48 hours Barry called me and explained that after thoroughly reviewing the materials he believed that Par Three Financial was perpetrating a large fraud. He told me to do two things. First, he asked that I introduced him to Par Three Financial as a potential investor, which I did immediately. Then he told me I would need to cooperate with three people from law enforcement—Peter Del Greco at the SEC in Los Angeles; Peter Norell from the FBI office in Santa Ana; and Karen Patterson from the California Department of Corporations. He assured me that these people could be trusted and needed to know the truth about my investment in Par Three Financial. Meanwhile, Par Three Financial is actively soliciting new investment capital from people across the country through ads in newspapers and their Web site. The company even offered current investors a commission for bringing in new investors.

Then, in only a matter of days, Barry submitted to me a detailed 32 page report addressed to law enforcement that he had written, which I am including as an addendum to this letter. The report proved to me beyond any doubt that Par Three Financial was a financial crime in progress. Barry went so far as to hire an outside expert in the banking industry who stated that Par Three's model was untenable. Barry asked me to not yet share the report with anyone and to continue to cooperate with law enforcement. He then said that I should create a reason to ask Par Three for my money back. He also reassured me and told me not to worry about my investment. "You will get your money back, Don. I promise," Barry would always say.

Simultaneously, Barry was promising the people at Par Three that he would invest his money once I received my money back. Although it took several weeks and many phone calls, the company returned my $200,000. I couldn't believe it!

The other $10,000 I invested through my IRA and I was told it would "take longer to process the paperwork." As soon as I got my $200,000 back, the Associated Press printed a story based on Barry's report questioning the Par Three Financial business model. Within weeks after that article, the company was shut down by the SEC, the FBI and the California Department of Corporations. It was then I discovered that there were investors all over the country and millions of dollars had been raised.

As it turns out, the person behind perpetrating the Par Three fraud was a convicted felon. What an irony. A convicted felon stole my money and a convicted felon got it back for me. If this didn't happen to me, I wouldn't have believed it.

Today my wife and I work with a court-appointed receiver in Florida to recover our final $10,000. However, that we were able [to recover] our $200,000 literally saved our financial lives. Which brings me to my last point.

Barry Minkow never charged me. He never asked me for any money. Even when I offered him money he did not accept it. And although to this day I don't know all the details as it relates to the question of "how," he promised me I would receive my money back—and I did. But other stories do not share such a happy ending. I applaud you Senator Kohl and the entire committee for asking the right question: how do we protect seniors?

My advice is threefold. First, we have obvious vulnerability. We do not want to outlive our savings and will therefore be forever vulnerable to these types of investment scams. So we invest out of fear and fear can cloud good judgment. Second, that law enforcement would follow the lead of Peter Del Greco, Peter Norell, and Karen Patterson and be more proactive in identifying, infiltrating, and shutting down these schemes.

Finally, please never underestimate the shame and embarrassment factor. We who have fallen for a scam may hide it from our kids out of sheer embarrassment. I know I had those feelings. I did not want to believe I had placed almost my entire life savings in a fraud. Disclosure is a real issue for those of us who fear how we may be perceived by our children.

I hope and pray that my experiences can help prevent the elderly from being victimized. I truly mean that. If I can answer any further questions, please do not hesitate to call me. I am not in good health so I cannot travel anymore, but I am available by phone. As for Barry Minkow, what he did for me will not make the front page of any newspaper. Funny isn't it? Had he perpetrated this Par Three fraud, the whole world would have known about it, but since he uncovered it and got an old man from Sequim, Washington his money back and proved that people can change—well,

I guess that's not much of a story. Thank you Senator Kohl and the others on the panel for making it one.

Respectfully submitted,
Don Scott

Step Three

WATCH THOSE TRIGGERS

Let us not say, Every man is the architect of his own for-
tune; but let us say, Every man is the architect of his own
character.

—GEORGE DANA BOARDMAN (1801–1831),
American missionary

C.S. Lewis once gave this great analogy about boating that will prove to be a critical tool for success for those who are coming back from failure. He said that whenever a captain of a ship sets out to sea he must ask himself three questions.

First, the captain must ask: "What am I doing out here in the first place?" Lewis related that to our purpose in life. Second, the captain must ask: "How do I keep from running into other ships?" For Lewis this meant the problem of getting along with other people relationally and how certain people's lack of this skill can be devastating. Finally, and most importantly for my purposes, is the third question: *"How do I keep from sinking?"*

This question deals with the real propensity, especially for those of us who have failed, to self-destruct, or "sink." For whatever reason, once one sets sail on the seas of comeback there appears to be a point and time where we revisit the very behavior that launched the initial failure. And I am convinced this occurs because of a failure to understand the problem of "triggers."

Triggers are situations, circumstances, and/or incidents that occur during the normal course of coming back from failure that provoke the temptation to revert back to those old habits that caused failure in the first place. In other words, we set out to sail on the seas of comeback only to sink, not from a hurricane or even another ship, but rather from our own, self-destructive sinking-type behavior.

The triggers I am referring to vary from person to person, but it is critical to identify them and be aware of our vulnerability to their allure when they arise—because it is inevitable that they will. Just when the past has become precisely that—the past—out of nowhere an unexpected incident or series of incidents will arise to upset the balance of your comeback. A trigger shifts the vehicle of our vulnerability into drive and sets in motion a series of bad decisions that can, if unchecked, ruin any comeback bid, and we sink . . . again.

Preparing for the triggers begins with first identifying them, which in my case should have been an easy task. However, experience taught me otherwise. For example, any real-life situation where I was faced with the choice of doing what was right versus what was expedient was a trigger that would tempt me into my old ways of dealing with things. Failing to prepare ahead of time for this trigger is simply inexcusable on my part.

Additionally, circumstances where my pride or ego were threatened or damaged were triggers for me to revert back to my old ways. When confronted with these types of situations in the past I would become manipulative and dishonest in an attempt to salvage my dignity and control others' opinion of me. And, of course, there were plenty of instances where the selfishness or the "meeting *my* needs" triggers appeared. There was a time that I never encountered a perceived need that I did not, legally or illegally, attempt to gratify.

A simple, honest inventory is the prescription for the trigger problem. My mistake was forgetting to fill the prescription so there were instances where I failed again.

—

"Barry, this is great news," Chris Roslan exclaimed. Chris was a longtime friend and partner in Dera, Roslan, and Campion, the public relations firm hired to do publicity on my autobiography *Cleaning Up*. "Steve Kroft from *60 Minutes* wants to begin filming right away and he says the segment will air sometime in May of 2005!" Chris' enthusiasm spilled through the phone into my joyful ear. The call came in late February 2005 after months of his hard work. When it came to competence in the public relations business, there is none better than Chris, and he was excited that *60 Minutes* wanted to do an update segment on the onetime whiz kid of Wall Street who'd turned undercover fraud investigator for the Feds.

I am not happy to admit I already had some experience with *60 Minutes*. In 1987, Diane Sawyer did a story on the fall of ZZZZ Best that was anything but flattering. She eventually moved on to ABC but not before she portrayed me as the worst crook of the 1980s. I would be angry and bitter but for the fact that she was so accurate!

Then, in 2003, a producer from *60 Minutes* contacted me out of the blue and indicated that they were interested in doing an update story on me, which would focus on the first fraud case I was working on uncovering. I had just been written up in the *Wall Street Journal* and the story indicated that I was working on uncovering a fraud case. That case was MX Factors, a factoring company that was offering investors a quarterly return of 12 percent. At the time the producer of *60 Minutes* called, I was trying, with the help of two outstanding private investigators (Juan Lopez and Paul Palladino), to convince law enforcement that the company was an elaborate Ponzi scheme. (The company was shut down in September of 2003.)

My initial failure was a national news event; would my comeback be one as well? I jumped at the opportunity to have *60 Minutes* do a follow-up story sixteen years later that would seemingly redeem my public image. The producer sent crews out to San Diego to film the church during one of my sermons and to conduct several preinterviews. However, just as quickly as this story was born, it died. The day after the *60 Minutes* crew left San Diego, I received a call from the producer indicating that "the timing was not right for this type of story," and despite having invested both time and money, they cancelled the segment. Needless to say, I was disappointed because it appeared that this story, unlike the one that aired in 1987 covering my fraud at ZZZZ Best, would actually be positive.

Two years later it appeared that the timing was better, and I received the call from Chris Roslan. At that time there were about ten fraud cases that we had successfully uncovered, and with that kind of track record the *60 Minutes* producers believed the comeback story was now worth telling. The producers assigned to the story were Graham Messick and Joel Patterson, who would work with Steve Kroft. The producers were extremely thorough as they sought to independently corroborate everything I had said or had done. Many years ago such scrutiny would have signaled my downfall. However, when you are *not* trying to conceal a fraud within a public company, such an investigation is painless.

After almost four weeks of numerous e-mails back and forth between the producers and me, preinterviews, hundreds of phone calls, and documents confirming the fraud cases, Joel Patterson phoned with the bad news. He indicated that the upper brass at *60 Minutes* was, once again, considering canceling the story. But before my heart sank completely into my stomach, he explained a way in which the story could be salvaged. Joel asked if I had any current fraud cases in which *60 Minutes* could actually follow me with a hidden camera so that they could capture for themselves my methodology in identifying and uncovering financial fraud.

Initially, I considered all the obstacles with such a suggestion. First is the issue that white-collar crime, in general, is not overly exciting. In fact, much of the work that is done in uncovering these types of crimes is performed behind the scenes. Unlike the thrill of catching a bank robber in the middle of a crime, white-collar crime investigation is much more meticulous and requires hours of public records searches, interviews with investors and industry experts, and site visits in an effort to find inconsistencies with what the "promoter" (or perpetrator) is promising investors and the actual reality.

But the biggest problem with the *60 Minutes* request was my relationship with law enforcement. When I worked under-cover with the FBI to expose a fraud, I was not permitted to leak information to the media, nor was I allowed to talk to the press about an ongoing case. In the case of Derek Turner and his $500-million hedge fund, I worked with law enforcement for eighteen months and was told more than once that if I talked to the media I would jeopardize the entire investigation. I honored their request, and Turner ended up being sentenced to twenty years in prison after a successful multicountry investigation.

Thus, the two challenges I faced with complying with the *60 Minutes* request was (1) the fact that white-collar crime was difficult to capture on film and (2) permitting the media to enter the world of an ongoing undercover operation, which is strictly forbidden by law enforcement. However, when Joel Patterson indicated that the story might not be "interesting enough" to air without the component of an undercover angle, I panicked. I just could not allow this story to have the same fate as the story of 2003.

I racked my brain searching for options and then it hit me. Although I could not allow the *60 Minutes* cameras to follow me undercover in an *ongoing* law enforcement investigation, I could take them with me on a case that I had not yet referred to law enforcement. I quickly concluded that the only thing that separated me from appearing on *60 Minutes* was a new fraud case that I could investigate myself, allow *60 Minutes* to tag along, and then submit to law enforcement. That would produce a happy ending for all of us—except the perpetrator, of course. In this scenario, my actions would technically be acceptable because I was not bringing *60 Minutes* on, let's say, the Par Three Financial fraud case, which I had submitted to law enforcement a month earlier. Three branches of law enforcement were actively investigating that case at the time.

That was the moment I remembered that I had been recently contacted by a man who was concerned that his close friend and fellow church attendee had just donated half a million dollars on behalf of his church to a "matching grant program" that promised him (and the church) a 100 percent return on the money within one year. According to the man who contacted me, the promoters promised that every quarter 25 percent of their principal investment (in this case, the half mil) would be returned, so that within one year the investors would receive their principal money and have $500,000 in "profit" or matched contribution to the non-profit entity of their choice—preferably Christian. The only condition was the church or someone on the church's behalf had to first put the $500,000 in an escrow account that the promoter would have access to but promised "not to use" for the full year; then and only then would the promoters match the funds over that one-year time period.

Typically in cases like the above, I would begin a three-pronged process of qualifying the lead. First, I would research whether or not this particular case or investment deal was something that fell into our field of expertise and whether there was probable cause that a financial crime was being committed. Second, I'd call the FBI to make sure that they were not already investigating the company and/or person. I would then share in a brief e-mail and with some minimal supporting documentation the basis for why I had concluded probable cause existed for further investigation. Finally, and only if the case passed the first two tests, I would seek permission from either Special Agent Supervisor Peter Norell or Special Agent Matt Galioto to infiltrate the alleged fraud by posing as a prospective investor, with the understanding that I would immediately provide my findings to the FBI and other relevant law enforcement agencies like the SEC or state regulators.

This process had served me well over the past two years. It kept me away from cases that were not in my area of expertise, which enabled me (more by luck than skill) to maintain a perfect record in identifying financial crimes in progress. Also, in turn, the careful qualification process boosted the Fraud Discovery Institute's credibility with law enforcement. However, the one thing I could not afford to do was jeopardize this relationship with law enforcement by violating their trust in me. In fact, I remember one FBI agent telling me at a fraud conference I was teaching that the only reason I, as a convicted felon, had any influence with the FBI was not necessarily because of my ability to identify and work undercover to expose financial crimes in progress, but rather because I had never asked an agent or supervisor for any special favors or money for my services. So much for my thinking I was a great investigator!

After reading through the materials on the matching grant program, I recognized many points of similarity with the New Era Philanthropy fraud case of 1989. This was both good and bad news. Bad for the people in the matching grant program but good for me in that the case appeared to be a fraud—and I was in need of one at the time. (The thing about fraud perpetrators that has always amazed me is we seldom come up with new schemes, just variations on old ones!)

In the New Era Philanthropy fraud perpetrated by John G. Bennett, Jr., donors were promised that in six months' time Bennett would double the investment of any nonprofit organization that gave him money—meaning if a church gave him $100,000, within six months that church would receive $200,000 in return. Such returns, Bennett claimed, were made possible by wealthy philanthropists who wanted to make anonymous donations to charities through New Era. One of the red flags that eventually led to the demise of New Era Philanthropy was Bennett's insistence that charitable organizations first turn over their money in order to receive money from New Era. This was the key point of similarity in the case that I was now examining.

I then contacted Peter Norell and Matt Galioto and explained the situation with the matching grants and my preliminary findings. They both indicated that the FBI had no current, ongoing investigation. Instead of replying, "Great, is it OK if I infiltrate this alleged scheme and report my findings back to you?" I said nothing. I immediately called the producers of *60 Minutes* and promised that I would be able to deliver on their requirement to follow me as I uncovered a financial crime in progress. Needless to say, they were elated.

Now it was time to move into action. First, I had to get the person who initially contacted me to introduce me to the promoters of the deal as a prospective investor desiring to have a grant matched on behalf of his church. Since I was also the pastor of a church, my guise as a potential investor fit perfectly. The ideal setting for *60 Minutes* was to have me wear a hidden camera to a meeting with the matching grant promoters and record the pitch in which I would be enticed to put a certain amount of money into an "escrow account" for a year, so that each quarter the promoters would be able to match 25 percent of my principal investment. As I had hoped, everything worked as planned and the promoters asked that I meet with them in Dallas, Texas, on 24 March 2005. Joel Patterson and Graham Messick were elated and explained that this was the first undercover story *60 Minutes* had approved in years.

However, there were other obstacles that I feared but shared with no one. In every fraud case I had investigated, I always faced the very real possibility of what I call the "I could be wrong" issue. In this case, if I was wrong about this matching grant program, if for some reason this turned out to be a legitimate operation and the promoters failed to make representations to me that were not true, I would look like an idiot on national television!

This potential downside prompted me to try to make sure I was sure. To do this, I personally tracked down Albert Meyer, the CPA who had uncovered the New Era Philanthropy fraud, and asked him if I was on the right track with this case. After reviewing the materials and the initial report I had put together, he issued a 'To whom it may concern' letter agreeing with my findings that this matching grant program appeared to be a fraud similar to the case he'd uncovered. I felt better. Let me tell you, justification takes lot of legwork!

The other issue was the law enforcement dilemma. In every case up until this time, I had openly shared information with the FBI on the approach I would take to secure documents from the promoters, what I intended to do in terms of specific money I would offer to invest in the deal, and disclosure of any scheduled meetings, in case they wanted to record those meetings for evidence in a potential criminal filing. As I flew from San Diego to Dallas to attend the meeting with the matching grant promoters, I realized, albeit far too late, that I had a problem with a trigger.

———

The trigger that set my manipulative mind into action was not big Wall Street dollars, as in the case of ZZZZ Best, but rather the more subtle allure of an ego gratifying appearance on *60 Minutes*—to the extent that any *60 Minutes* appearance could be ego gratifying! The truth was, I simply did not want to lose the opportunity to be portrayed as a "good guy" helping expose an apparent ongoing fraud on the very show that had previously exposed me as the fraud that I was (and then, years later, cancelled the segment that would have redeemed me).

Because of this desire, I found myself rationalizing and justifying what I knew to be wrong, just as I had done years before at ZZZZ Best. Granted, the justifications this time were not to steal millions of dollars to meet payroll for a public company that secretly owed money to the Mob, but the principle was the same. The trigger that had occurred years before had resurfaced again— albeit in a different context—and I was unprepared.

To make myself feel better and justify my manipulative actions, I remember thinking back to the many hours I had put into the various cases I had uncovered over the past two years without pay. *Even drug dealers who turn snitch get paid by the FBI as informants*, I thought to myself. *And I get nothing*. I thought about the many threats that always accompanied proactive fraud discovery. Inevitably, once the promoter of an investment fraud found out that I was not a potential investor but rather the impetus that helped bring down the scheme, threats would sometimes follow. These threats caused my wife great hardship even though I convinced myself not to worry about them.

I also considered potential book sales and how an appearance on *60 Minutes* would most certainly benefit me financially. Finally, there was the impact of the pride and ego that accompanied the possibility of correctly identifying a financial crime in progress on a national television show.

But mitigating factors were also racing through my mind. Matt Galioto and Peter Norell, against the better judgment of many naysayers within the FBI, had believed in me and always supported my efforts at making good through uncovering various frauds. They never lied to me nor withheld information about an investigation. Most importantly, after working hundreds of hours with them, they had actually become my friends.

Matt Galioto and Peter Norell's official position regarding the Fraud Discovery Institute was simple: for whatever reason, people were clearly contacting me first before they were contacting law enforcement about serious financial crimes totaling millions of dollars and impacting thousands of victims. Both of them wanted to follow up on that information. Perhaps it was the appearance of bureaucracy that prevented people from contacting law enforcement first, but to Matt and Peter it mattered little. They had only one goal and that was to save people and the public in general from being defrauded, whether they got the credit for it or not.

Yet here I was on a plane to Dallas going undercover with a Nielsen top-ten-rated television show to expose a fraud that I had not first disclosed to the FBI. The producers of *60 Minutes* were not concerned because great journalism often attempts to proactively uncover wrongdoing. If this undercover operation proved that people were being defrauded, the *60 Minutes* team was committed to bringing those involved to justice by cooperating with law enforcement. The issue was Barry Minkow, not *60 Minutes*. I could have told the *60 Minutes* team that even though we were doing nothing wrong and the operation would probably bring a financial crime to light, I owed law enforcement first right of refusal. But because I had a need I wanted met, pride and ego to feed, and money to make from book sales, I did not want to take the chance. So I said nothing.

"I'm sorry, Matt," I apologized when I returned from Dallas. I knew I would have to call him and explain what I had done. "I realize that it was wrong and deceptive of me to not disclose the fact that *60 Minutes* was following me to Dallas."

"I appreciate the call, Barry. However, we knew about the undercover video in Dallas because *60 Minutes* told us. They were calling about your other cases and mentioned it," Matt explained. I did not know how to respond.

"Look Barry, technically we cannot control you or what you do. You are not an employee of the FBI and we do not even pay you as a contractor. And we appreciate the help you have offered. But I think you need to call Pete Norell. He's a little more taken back about this than I am," Matt said firmly. I apologized for my actions and promised Matt that this would not happen again. He was kind and forgiving, but it was obvious that what I did affected him. I dutifully called Peter Norell.

"Well, if it isn't the Bureau's new PR director. Great to talk to you, Barry," Peter stated with a hint of sarcasm. I knew what he meant. I just listened. "There is one FBI office that I recommend you do not contact anytime soon. The Dallas FBI office is not too happy with an apparent financial crime in their jurisdiction that they did not know about. And then to come to find out that one of our own cooperators took a *60 Minutes* crew with him? Not a great scenario."

Rarely am I lost for words. Peter Norell was the kind of guy that a perpetrator would make the mistake of underestimating. Like Matt Galioto, he was not a self-promoter. He did, however, stay on top of the white-collar-crime industry, as evidenced by his never taking more than about two minutes to comprehend even the most complex fraud cases.

"I'm sorry Pete. And you can bet it will not happen again." He said nothing. "I will also forward you the transcripts of that meeting in case you need them for any future prosecution."

"How were you able to get those?" Pete asked. This time, I said nothing. "Send them to me," he ordered. "And one more thing. My fear for Barry Minkow is not that you will run a publicly held company again or some kind of hedge fund where you will lie to the public and steal their money. My real concern for you is that you will make the mistake of doing what you do for law enforcement to make the headlines—not because you believe that it is the right thing to do. If your life experience has taught you anything, it should have taught you that what people think of you matters little when you have to violate a principle to earn their approval."

On Sunday 22 May 2005, *60 Minutes* aired its segment on me and the undercover sting in Dallas. The segment included a brief interview with my former federal judge, Dickran Tevrizian, who spoke very highly of me, and an independent expert *60*

Minutes had hired to review the fraud report I issued on the alleged Ponzi Scheme in Dallas. The expert agreed with my findings and, right on the air, complimented my work. The only negative part of the story was when Steve Kroft mentioned my first book, *Cleaning Up.*

Remember the book sales I wanted so badly that I held back information from law enforcement? Steve Kroft reported, "But Barry still has not lost his flair for self-promotion as evidenced by his new book, *Cleaning Up.*" Ouch. "Flair for self-promotion." He had to go there on national television. I remember watching that part of the episode and thinking, *I wonder how he knew. . . .*

———

I first met Arthur Smith, Kent Weed, and Sean Atkins in late 2004. They own the popular television production company, A. Smith and Company, known for such hits as *Hell's Kitchen* and *Paradise Hotel,* among others. They were introduced to me through the William Morris Agency, a talent agency who represented me primarily for things like writing books (yes, even this one) and speaking engagements. A. Smith and Company were also clients of the agency.

The production company initiated contact because they wanted to create some kind of television show based on my life . . . or at least loosely based on my life. They invented several clever scenarios that could possibly become television shows. One idea was a Barry Minkow reality show that would follow me as I attempted to uncover fraud, a similar idea to the *Dog the Bounty Hunter* show on A&E. They also tossed around the idea of a scripted one-hour drama that would examine the life of an ex-convict who by day pastored a church but by night became an undercover fraud investigator for the FBI.

This was not my first introduction to Hollywood. Years earlier, another production company, Fisher/Merlis Television, had approached me to put together a similar show. Their emphasis was a daily thirty-minute fraud-awareness show that would be hosted by yours truly. It would be less about the exposure of fraud, because at that time in my life I had not uncovered any financial crimes. What I remembered most about my experience with George Merlis and Albert Fisher was not only their kindness and love, but also how much they really believed that a show like the one we were pitching to network buyers would actually help people avoid becoming victims of fraud—in an entertaining way.

Shows and movies get sold in Hollywood as agents set up meetings for their clients with buyers like NBC, CBS, ABC, or syndicators like Kingworld, Buena Vista, or Telepicture, or even cable networks like USA and FX. That is exactly what George, Albert, and I did from 1997 to 2000. We traipsed from meeting to meeting, pitching our television show concept for the buyers to consider. We met with every network, every syndicator, and every cable network that we thought would want this kind of programming. Every meeting was like being stuck in a bad episode of *The Twighlight Zone*. Here's the script.

- The buyers of this type of programming would always agree to meet with us.

- I would motor up from San Diego to Los Angeles to take the meeting with my adrenalin pumping and my hopes soaring.

- George, Albert, and I would be handed a nice beverage and treated with respect.

- The meeting always went better than expected with parting comments like, "We will call you back soon— great idea for a show."

- On the way to our cars afterward, George, Albert, and I were always convinced that this was the company or network that would break the chain of nos and instead say yes.

- I'd turn my car back toward San Diego, not minding the 405 freeway traffic, with confidence that we would get a yes within days.

- After arriving at home, a disappointed George or Albert would call with condolences. The buyer had said no. Again. Review this list over and over and you might have an idea of how I felt three years later.

After the year 2000, George, Albert, and I stayed friends but gave up our efforts to sell this kind of show. However, my experience with these men—men who spent hours with me and never made a nickel but never lost confidence or faith in me—will impact me forever. "That's the business we are in, Barry," they would always say with big grins. "Please don't feel bad for us."

So when, in the summer of 2005, I embarked after almost six months of preparation to sell the new show concept with A. Smith and Company, I knew things would be different. Now I had a long track record uncovering frauds and I was with a production company that was at the top of its game with several hit shows under its belt.

But because I remembered the past, when the four of us (Sean, Arthur, Kent, and myself) began pitching the show I told them never to accept a cold beverage at any of these pitch meetings. "If they give you the beverage—even if it's just water, it means they are definitely going to say no and are just trying to be nice to us by giving us something to drink," I reasoned. "It's how they lessen the blow of no." The three of them just looked at me and shook their heads, kind of like parents do when their child has done something so outrageous that no adjectives, only a cursory headshake, could express how they feel.

During the late summer and early fall of 2005 we pitched everyone. Each meeting's outcome was another no. Whom we met with didn't matter. Networks, cable, syndicators . . . everyone said no. Our comprehensive list also included companies that had purchased shows from A. Smith and Company before! We even tried not drinking the beverage that was inevitably offered at each of these meetings but, much to my dismay we still got the proverbial no. When the season concluded at the end of 2005, we tried again in the late spring of 2006 with a new show concept: *Convict Court*. This show was a take-off on popular judge shows like *Judge Judy*. The twist was having me, a convicted felon, act as the judge. I actually liked this idea and, by filming five shows in one day I would be able to, with some adjustments, still balance the rest of my life as a pastor and fraud investigator.

But once again, everywhere we went, we got a no. I felt bad— not for me but for Arthur, Kent, and Sean, who invested tons of time and money for almost two years with no return. And, like

Albert and George, they never wavered in their belief in me. They told me not to take rejection personally and that more than 95 percent of the shows that get pitched are rejected. And then, out of nowhere, I got a yes.

"So basically, Barry, we want to do this show and we want you to be the host," she explained. The call had taken me by surprise. I remembered pitching this particular buyer but did not expect her to call me personally. "The downside is we have a different production company that we want to use for the show." There was a long pause on the phone as I tried to understand exactly what she meant. Better to let her explain it in plain English.

"Meaning?" I asked.

"Meaning A. Smith and Company cannot do this show for us," she said flatly.

"But I am under contract with A. Smith and Company for a few more months," I interjected.

"Don't worry, when the time comes we can buy them out. It's done all the time in this business. Let us know." *Click.*

I slowly hung up the phone and contemplated the yes. For almost ten years I had waited to hear those words and finally someone had said, "I want you. I want to invest the time, energy, and effort to do a show that you will host."

All the other networks and syndicators that had told me no would look silly for their oversight of my potential on TV. I could earn enough money to pay back my last remaining ZZZZ Best debt—Union Bank. What a positive impact a successful television show might have upon the church or, better yet, my earning potential! I jumped out of my chair, barely able to control my enthusiasm and called my wife, Lisa, to share the news.

I spent about ten minutes telling Lisa about the two-minute call, the yes, and the potential. She only had one question, "What about A. Smith and Company?"

To appreciate this question you must know Lisa. She is an uncomplicated person. She does not see the world as I do. She is not manipulative and is often taken advantage of by people because she always assumes the best about them and leaves herself vulnerable. To her, right and wrong are constants not determined by a given situation. She was the one who would benefit greatly if I were to do a television show because that would mean more income for the household. But as evidenced by her first reaction to what I said, Lisa is not about money as much as she is about people. That is why she is just as comfortable accompanying me as I preach at a prison or a rescue mission as she is going to a five-star hotel and to meet a politician or a television celebrity.

It took only those six words from Lisa to slam everything back into perspective for me. This was not a television issue, this was a trigger issue. Legally I could probably agree to do this show and finally live the big yes. Morally I would be abandoning the people who believed in me just for another shot at fame. It was really the *60 Minutes* issue all over again—repackaged with only a few differences. Greed, pride, ego, and fame were all present in their usual appealing garb, but this time I determined that the outcome would be different. A lot different.

Hours after I had spoken to Lisa, I called Sean Atkins at A. Smith and Company and told him about the offer and asked that he keep the information confidential and only between us. As I recounted for him the conversation with the lady, I gave specific details about the new show and proposed production company—details that I would have known only if I was telling the truth.

"What are you going to do, Barry?" he asked hesitantly.

Before he finished speaking I blurted, "I'm going to say no." Sean did not respond. "And I am going to say no because of those damn triggers." He did not know what I meant. But Lisa did. I did. So for the first time in my life I actually made the correct decision when presented with a trigger and I did not sink.

A month later while on a conference call with Arthur, Kent, and Sean, Arthur mentioned that he wanted to go pitch the very company that had called me with a show offer that did not include A. Smith and Company. I immediately said no, which led to the "why no" question. That is when Sean spoke up. He quickly recounted to Kent and Arthur the series of events that had transpired between me and this company. After he explained what had happened and that I had said no, Arthur said something that made me smile for weeks: "Wow, Barry. That's not what usually happens in Hollywood. I always knew that you had changed and now you just proved me right."

———

Remember the classic movie *Gone with the Wind* and the character Scarlett O'Hara (played by Vivian Leigh)? Her words are worth remembering: "Tomorrow is another day." In that one line, Scarlett summed up what I have been trying to convey in this chapter. Yes, my past (and perhaps yours) was bad. Trying to suggest otherwise would be downright dishonest.

To deal with the past, some try to put as many miles as possible between them and their history. They move to different states or cities and hope that somehow a new location will facilitate their comeback. But the problem with that approach is not only that wherever you go, you always end bringing *you* with you but also that those triggers that launched the events that led to the original failure follow you to that new location.

But those of us who choose to acknowledge that triggers arising in the daily routine of life carry potentially devastating consequences for us are forearmed. As hopeful and promising as a phrase like *Tomorrow is another day* is, without a proper and proactive identification of our triggers, failure is inevitable—because coming back from failure requires a lot more than a few inspirational quotes. It requires a commitment to understanding the pitfalls of pride, ego, greed, or any other trigger that evokes behavior that leads to failure. No one has learned this concept better than Dave Bliss.

After being hired to coach a Continental Basketball Association (CBA) team in North Dakota, Dave Bliss admitted, "I made a mistake and I'm grateful for the second chance. I'm humbled by what I did."[1] For those of you that understand geography better than sports, the CBA is the lowest rung of professional basketball. Considering that only a few short years ago Bliss was one of the rising stars in the college coaching ranks, it was hard to fathom anyone, much less Dave Bliss, being grateful for the opportunity to coach minor league basketball in North Dakota.

But sure enough, Bliss, through full disclosure of his triggers, learned from his past mistakes. He admitted, "Selfishness and ambition played a large role in what I did." What exactly did

Bliss do? Well, it's more about what he *didn't* do. When Patrick Dennehy was shot to death by his Baylor teammate Carlton Dotson, Coach Bliss became desperate. He was so afraid that his program's recruiting violations would be exposed in the investigation that he completely lost track of the line between right and wrong, decent and indecent.

Back then, Bliss actually urged his players to lie to police so they wouldn't discover that boosters paid Dennehy's tuition and rent. He even suggested players mislead the cops with rumors that Dennehy sold drugs to pay for school. But Bliss's lies eventually caught up to him (my experience at ZZZZ Best taught me that all too well) and he resigned from Baylor University in August 2003. In fact, Baylor's own internal investigation found that approximately forty thousand dollars had been given to Dennehy and another player, or spent on tuition. Additionally, members of the coaching staff were instructed to turn a blind eye to positive drug tests from star players.

How did Bliss defend these actions? He didn't. Instead he said, "I take full responsibility for what happened. You can only ask for forgiveness. I made a selfish decision to give those players scholarships. I don't want that to be my epitaph. I've been a good soldier and I've helped a lot of young people."[2] And he has. First, Bliss volunteered at a local high school in Colorado where his son was playing; later he went to China with a small group of NBA players. But he has no illusions about how tough this new job will be, despite his once stellar résumé.

"I'm a veteran in other circles, but I've got a lot to learn and I'm excited about adapting to a different environment . . . in any case, I'm just glad to be working." With that attitude, it won't be long before he gets another opportunity at the college level. Do you know why? Because the next time the trigger of selfish ambition rears its ugly head in Dave Bliss's life, he will be ready. And so will you—if you remember what a good captain does before he sails.

Step Four

PREPARE FOR CRITICISM . . . AND I MEAN REALLY PREPARE

The tragedy of life is what dies inside a man while he lives.
—ALBERT SCHWEITZER (1875–1965),
Nobel Peace Prize winner

On 22 January 1987, R. Budd Dwyer, who had been the Pennsylvania state treasurer for eight years, called a press conference a day before his sentencing to update people on his situation. He had been recently convicted of taking approximately three hundred thousand dollars in kickbacks and was facing up to fifty-five years in prison.

Mr. Dwyer, who had served in both houses of the state legislature of the Pennsylvania government, read a prepared speech stating the following:

I thank the good Lord for giving me forty-seven years of exciting challenges, stimulating experiences, many happy occasions, and, most of all, the finest wife and children any man could ever desire.

Several television stations throughout Pennsylvania were carrying this press conference live, unwittingly about to broadcast a catastrophe. Mr. Dwyer continued,

> We were confident that right and truth would prevail, and I would be acquitted and we would devote the rest of our lives working to create a justice system here in the United States. The guilty verdict has strengthened that resolve. But as we've discussed our plans to expose the warts of our legal system, people have said, "Why bother," "No one cares," "You'll look foolish," "60 Minutes, 20/20, the American Civil Liberties Union, Jack Anderson, and others have been publicizing cases like yours for years, and it doesn't bother anyone."[1]

With those final words, he abruptly ended his prepared speech, opened a large manila envelope and withdrew a .357 Magnum revolver. Cameras continued rolling and amidst shocked shouts pleading for him to reconsider, Mr. Dwyer swallowed the barrel of the gun, pulled the trigger, and killed himself on live television.

———

On 24 January 2002, Clifford Baxter, the former vice chairman of the Enron Corporation of Houston, Texas, went to sleep at 9:15 p.m. He slept until about 2:00 a.m. When he awoke, he loaded his Smith & Wesson .357 Magnum five-shot revolver, arranged some pillows under the covers, and wrote a brief suicide note, which he left in his wife's car. Baxter then drove his Mercedes a few blocks down Royale Boulevard and parked between two medians. At that fateful moment he shot himself in the head. His mutilated body was found inside the parked car at 2:23 a.m.

The suicide note he left behind spelled out the anguish leading to his action. "I am so sorry for this. I feel I just can't go on," the note read. "I've always tried to do the right thing, but where there was once great pride, now it's gone . . . the pain is overwhelming."[2]

———

The pitch . . . Deep to left and Downing goes back. And it's gone! Unbelievable! You're looking at one for the ages here. Astonishing! Anaheim Stadium was one strike away from turning into Fantasyland! And now the Red Sox lead six to five! The Red Sox get four runs in the ninth on a pair of two-run homers by Don Baylor and Dave Henderson.[3]

On 12 October 1986 in Anaheim, the Angels held a three-games-to-one lead of a best-of-seven against the Boston Red Sox. The Angels held a 5–2 lead going into the ninth inning when Boston scored two runs on a hit by Bill Buckner and a home run by Don Baylor, closing the gap to 5–4.

Relief pitcher Donnie Moore was sent in by the Angels to shut down the rally with two outs, and with Rich Gedman on first base. The Angels were one out shy of making it to the World Series.

The game went into extra innings, and at the top of the eleventh inning the Red Sox were able to score off Moore via a sacrifice fly by Henderson. The Angels were unable to score in the bottom of the eleventh and lost the game 7–6.

This defeat still left the Angels with a three-to-two game advantage, with two more games left to play at Fenway Park. But when the Angels lost both games by wide margins, Moore was ultimately blamed for the shortcoming.

He had battled depression for some time. And his unhealthy combination of drug abuse and alcoholism lead to serious difficulties in his marriage. The media and sports fans hounded him mercilessly for the Angels' loss, and he was unable to recover from his depression.

On 18 July 1989, Moore ended a heated argument with his wife Tonya by shooting her three times, witnessed by their three children. Tonya Moore and daughter Demetria, then seventeen years of age, fled from the house in terror. Although Demetria was able to drive her mother to the hospital in time to save her life, back inside the house, Moore's rage consumed him. In the presence of one of his sons, Moore turned the gun on himself. He died of a self-inflicted wound at the age of thirty-five.[4]

———

I wrote this book because of stories like these. I'm sad to say that I'm sure there are many, many more. All too often people who have experienced the debilitating emotional pain of public failure—deserved or not—have chosen to simply avoid any attempt at comeback. Unfortunately, they instead choose to "opt out" with suicide. The primary motivator for this is the overwhelming feeling of hopelessness that always accompanies failure.

Putting a face on hopelessness is not a difficult task—not for someone like me.

- After what I have done, no one will ever trust me again.

- No matter what I do with the rest of my life, I will always be remembered for my failures.

- Why even bother trying when nothing will ever really be the same for me again?

Although I cannot read the minds of those who have sadly and prematurely ended their lives after a failure, I would be willing to bet the concerns listed above were at least a part of their reasoning process. Unfortunately, they are also accurate depictions of what awaits those of us who have failed. It would be disingenuous to fervently promise otherwise. Yes, failing, by definition is painful. *But it does not have to be fatal.*

I wish there were some motivational speech I could give that would somehow change the reality of how difficult things will be for people who have failed. I wish I could change the perception of those who will always adhere to the age-old axioms of "a leopard doesn't change its spots" or "people never change." I wish I could infiltrate every human resources department of the Fortune 500 companies and explain why hiring people who have failed will improve productivity. As I argued in step one, given that second chance, no one will ever work harder than a person who has been given an opportunity to prove himself.

But the truth of the matter is this: *failure, like puckered scars from old wounds, will always be a part of us.* Simply stated, people will be quick to remind us of our past mistakes—no matter how much time has passed or how sincere our motives are. And the way to deal with coming back from failure is to not dilute or ignore this reality.

Similarly, using this predictive rejection and skepticism of others, perhaps even family members, as an excuse to opt out of coming back from failure is not an option either—especially once one is prepared. Herein lies the reason I wrote this book: to prepare and equip, inspire and encourage a generation of people like me who have made certain decisions during various and diverse circumstances that eventually led (remember the Principle of the Path) to devastation. And when we reached for the delete button for that part of our lives, there wasn't one. Now we are stuck with the inescapable reality of our decisions and actions. *But all is not lost. The remaining chapters of your life have yet to be written.*

YOU DO NOT BEGIN AGAIN AT "NEUTRAL"

On Friday, 12 May 2006, the sports section of the *San Diego Union Tribune* carried a story about an HBO Real Sports interview with former quarterback Ryan Leaf, done by Bernie Goldberg. Leaf had been the second overall pick of the San Diego Chargers in the 1998 NFL draft. By all accounts, his career never met the expectations many had set for him and now, sadly, some even consider him to be the greatest bust in NFL history.

But the one thing that jumped out at me from this article was Goldberg's observation about *why* Ryan Leaf failed. Goldberg perceived the reason after watching an embarrassing exchange and confrontation between Leaf and a reporter immediately following a game in which Leaf had played poorly. In commenting on that particular encounter, Leaf told Goldberg that it was "the downfall of my career." Goldberg told the *Union Tribune* reporter that Leaf, to this day, did not know why he had failed. Goldberg's observations about Leaf were captured in the article:

> Had he [Leaf] gone out the next Sunday and thrown four touchdown passes against the Giants instead of four interceptions, no one would have cared that he yelled at a reporter. They would have been too busy cheering him. "In the world of big-time sports, nothing is as important as winning," Goldberg said. "He could have said what he said to you—or to your mother—and it wouldn't have mattered." Goldberg said when he viewed the tape of the incident again recently, he was struck not by Leaf's words (there were only 10), but the "utter frustration" on his part. *It occurred to me that we're talking about a guy who never learned how to deal with failure . . . Most of us have failed over the years, where something bad happens, but you know how to deal with it.*[5]

What a great observation! Goldberg said that after failing badly in a game and receiving criticism, it shook Leaf so much the he went into a downward spiral that he not was able to pull out of for the duration of his career. The reason for that is that while playing college ball for the Washington State Cougars, he averaged over 330 yards per game in the twenty-four games that he started as quarterback and led the school to their first Rose Bowl appearance in sixty-seven years.

Translation? He had never really failed. So when he reached the NFL and did fail in a game, he experienced the sharp criticism that always accompanies failing. And Leaf was not prepared to respond verbally or on the field. According to Goldberg, this more than anything else contributed to his demise in the NFL.

In like manner, those of us who have failed must realize a crucial reality about its consequences—specifically that we do not start out neutral in the eyes of others. We cannot naively assume we do. The fact is, we start out with one or two strikes against us because the cognitive template people use when evaluating us changes once our past failures are revealed. That is, that standard mental process that employers, society, the media, and people in general use alters when they become aware of our past mistakes. The bigger the mistakes, the more scrutiny and criticism one can expect to endure. This more than anything else is the reason people who have failed too often choose to actively opt out through suicide or passively opt out by never fully recovering from a past failure.

I am convinced, after almost twenty years on the comeback trail, that the greatest obstacle to coming back from failure is not a lack of creativity or ambition. It is not a lack of intellect or business savvy or even love. The greatest obstacle to coming back from failure is *not being adequately prepared to face an all-out offensive on our present selves based on our past bad acts by people we will inevitably encounter on the journey forward.*

Is this reality fair? Of course not, but do not make the mistake of confusing what is *fair* with what is *true*. Just ask Bill Buckner. In a career that began with the Los Angeles Dodgers, Buckner collected over 2,700 hits, had a career average of .289, and won a National League batting title. Yet he will always be remembered for one terrible moment in the 1986 World Series when a ball went through his legs on a routine grounder while he was playing first base, and his team, the Red Sox, ended up losing to the Mets. One play, which probably took all of twenty seconds, is remembered more than a stellar twenty-two-year career.

Of course this bias is not fair, but it is true. The danger of not disclosing this ugly reality early and often in the comeback process is the moral equivalent of a doctor telling a cancer patient that chemotherapy and radiation will have no adverse side affects on his hair. In both instances, the person who has failed and the patient receiving the treatment will have real-life experiences that will be contrary to what they were *not* told—which can permanently damage an already fragile emotional state.

Consider the example of Sam E. Antar, a man who was no stranger to notoriety. A few years back, he and I struck up a friendship. Mr. Antar is an Orthodox Jew, and he initially contacted me to question how a man (me) who was raised Jewish could be a pastor of an evangelical church. Our discussions developed into a genuine friendship and, despite the fact that he lives in New York and I live in San Diego, we communicate frequently. I have truly grown to love and respect him.

Sam E. Antar was the chief financial officer for Crazy Eddie, Inc. During the 1980s he, along with his cousin Eddie Antar and his uncle Sam M. Antar, masterminded one of the largest securities fraud cases of its time. In fact, Crazy Eddie Antar was coined "the Darth Vader of Capitalism" by then-US Attorney Michael Chertoff.

Crazy Eddie became a household name in the late 1980s because of its now-famous over-the-top national television spots, which peddled everything from stereos to sound equipment. However, a $100 million fraud was the dirty truth behind the advertising at Crazy Eddie. When the fraud finally came to light, Sam E. Antar took a different approach than his cousin and his uncle. While Eddie and his uncle Sam denied any wrongdoing and failed to accept responsibility for their actions (Eddie even became a fugitive from justice), Sam E. Antar decided on an alternative approach: to accept responsibility.

He came to grips with the "it's all about me" step for coming back from failure and owned his past behavior by pleading guilty to his crimes—something I was not man enough to do, as evidenced by my four-and-a-half-month criminal trial. Moreover, Sam E. Antar helped the government trace embezzled money so the victims of the crime could recover some of their losses. This decision to own up to his actions did not come without a price; it rarely does. His entire family abandoned him and condemned him for "turning" on his cousin and uncle. To this day, many of them will not speak to him even though Eddie and Sam M. Antar (now deceased) were convicted of fraud.

Although the comeback road was a lonely one for Sam, he has traveled it with a clear conscience and without fear. He became determined to help future business executives avoid the trap of fraud by telling them his story—and did I mention he does this for free? If the formula *truth plus a long period of time equals trust* ever applied to anyone, it applies to Sam E. Antar. That is why I was surprised to read the e-mail below, which he sent me during a difficult time in his life.

——Original Message——
From: Sam E. Antar
Sent: Thursday, April 27, 2006 4:03 PM
To: info@frauddiscovery.net

Subject: Discrimination by Association

Barry:

There are people in this world that can never close the books on the past and want to constantly punish you. No matter how much redemption you do it is never enough. What is worse, they even target the people who associate with you and your family members. I believe it was Jesus who said, "Let he who hast not sinned the first sin, cast the first stone." Recently, _____[a company] dropped three refinance loans just three days prior to closing after almost $100,000 in expense and three months work, solely on the basis of me being married to a minority owner of three of the properties and the CFO of the management company that managed the three properties. (They had the right to choose another management company and still make the loan.) They alleged no fraud or misrepresentation as they dropped the loan in the 11th hour.

I am not asking for help, as this is just a commentary. I do not believe my wife, children, and others, should be penalized for me.

Enclosed is a copy of the denial for Eddy and Robin Antar. It states that: "Sam E. Antar, a convicted felon, is a senior officer of the property manager for all three properties and has associations with certain principals in the borrowing entities. See results of Lexis-Nexis search, attached, on Sam E. Antar."

My point is when does punishment and ridicule end? When is the debt to society paid off? Do we ever become "full" citizens of this country again? Why does it have to affect those around us too?

If not, how can a moral human being reconcile that philosophy with the fact that one day they will meet their creator (and) ask forgiveness for their sins? God may ask did you forgive others for the sins they made upon you?

Best regards to you and your family and with deepest respect,

Sammy[6]

My heart went out to him when I read this e-mail. Although it's not the most comforting fact, the sad reality is that Sam E. Antar's experience is the rule rather than the exception. Meaning, most who fail will learn that no matter how many years separate them from their failure or no matter how many "good" things they have accomplished, they will not avoid the reopening of the wound. And not preparing ahead of time for this will yield devastating consequences. To emphasize the importance of this point, here is how I answered three of Sammy's questions from his e-mail:

Sammy's question: When does punishment and ridicule end?

My answer: It never ends, Sammy. Take it from me, and like it or not, we who have failed will always find someone willing to assume the worst about us. And most of the time we do not have to look very far.

Sammy's question: When is the debt to society paid off?

My answer: In some people's eyes, Sammy, it is never paid off. As far as they are concerned, whatever your failure was (in my case the ZZZZ Best fraud and your case the Crazy Eddie fraud), you have committed the "unforgivable" sin.

Sammy's question: Why does it have to affect those around us too?

My answer: Because, Sammy, failure casts a wide net. Regrettably, the fact that our loved ones (children and parents included) may have had nothing to do with our past bad acts does little to shield them from sharing in our consequences.

But here's the good news. Here is the response that I have learned through my experience in rebounding from failure. This response is neither profound nor some deep theological truth that I have unearthed through some imputed esoteric knowledge. However, it is inherently practical and the single greatest piece of advice I have to offer to those who will experience ridicule and doubt on their journey back from failure. And that advice is? Who cares!

Did you miss that? Let me repeat it again for emphasis.

Who cares? I grant the premise that obstacles and ridicule potentially await me around every turn and yet my reaction is the same: *Who cares?* Now this is not an apathetic "who cares" that attempts to depreciate the significance of the impact of my failure on those I have hurt; but rather, this is an internal reminder that there are people, some in positions of power, that I will encounter who will not believe my commitment to comeback no matter what I say or do. I have reserved the big "who cares" for them.

Who cares what other people may think of our comeback ambition? Who cares that other people may doubt our motives, scrutinize our lives, and ridicule our dreams? I certainly don't—at least not anymore. After being on the front lines of the comeback battle here is my advice: Refuse to take your cues from those who are willing to believe the worst about you without first giving you the chance to prove otherwise.

Forfeiting our perceived right to have everyone love us and believe in us is both liberating and life-changing. When coming back from failure, focus on fighting the battles you can win, not on those you will most certainly lose. I learned this truth by realizing that even when I did have big money back in my heyday (a Ferrari, a public company, television commercials, appearances on *Oprah*, and all the perks associated with having money and fame) and long before the world knew I was a crook, not everyone liked Barry Minkow, despite how hard I tried to get them to do so.

The truth of the matter is a "win" in coming back from failure is not measured by popularity or how many people we are able to convince that change has occurred in our lives. A win is defined by the ability to not allow criticism, ridicule, gossip, and rejection thwart your comeback bid. Failing today or in the past does not guarantee the future will hold the same result for us—no matter what anybody says. As any mutual fund manager or stockbroker will tell you, *past performance is never a guarantee for future returns.* The irony is that the same people who use this motto for making investment decisions fail to consistently apply it to those people in need of a second chance from their past bad performance. More about that later, but for now, here's another story about someone else who made a change in their life for the better.

There was a young captain in the regular army in the Oregon territory in 1854, and he had fallen into some bad

habits. He missed his wife; he missed his baby back in
Missouri. He was the quartermaster, the paymaster. On the
day when he was to distribute the pay, he was intoxicated.
His superior officer, rather a martinet, and a very strict
man, said, "All right. You have two options. One is to resign
your commission and the other is to go before a court-
martial." This individual resigned his commission. The
young captain, after having resigned his commission, went
to New York and fell penniless on the shores there.

Time passed—ten years now—and in 1864 an army
officer steps into the Willard Hotel in Washington. He is
holding a small boy by the hand. Rather indifferently, the
clerk spins the register around to him and says, "Please sign."
He signs and whirls the register back to the clerk. The clerk
is astonished, for on the register is written the name: *Ulysses
S. Grant and son.* Ten years before, dismissed from the army
for intoxication; now a lieutenant general and supreme com-
mander of the Armies of the Union.[7]

Between the times of his resignation and later success in the
Union Army, Grant fell on hard times. After leaving the army, his
wife's father bought the couple a small farm, and although Grant
built a cozy cabin, worked the land, and intended to make it a
permanent residence, he failed. Due to deteriorating health and
weak crop prices, Grant was forced to sell their farm and peddle
firewood in big city streets.

Can you imagine asking Grant about his future then? He was
only a few years shy of the most prominent position in the entire
country. Had he given up because of the failure during that tough

period of his life, this country might be a different place than it is today. *And that is why opting out of comeback can never be an option.* You have no idea what great things may lie ahead—and if you quit because you do not comprehend the fact that we who fail do not begin in neutral but rather with strikes against us, you will never discover those great things! Those strikes do not determine your potential or your path. You do.

James Asperger, the former United States attorney who prosecuted me for the ZZZZ Best fraud, recommended to Judge Tevrizian to sentence me to twenty-five years (which the judge did). Fifteen years later, I requested that he write something for the back cover of my autobiography. During our conversation, he admitted he never would have believed that on my sentencing day in March of 1989 that he would later write the following endorsement:

> As Barry Minkow's prosecutor, I zealously prosecuted him
> for his crimes relating to the ZZZZ Best fraud. With that
> same zeal, Barry has made a remarkable turnaround—both
> in his personal life and in uncovering far more fraud than he
> ever perpetrated.

Had I quit because I listened to the many people along the way that doubted everything from my sincerity, to my conversion experience, to the reasons why I uncover fraud (and many still do but, well, who cares), I would never have experienced the joy that accompanies perseverance.

As for Grant, those traumatic years between the resignation and military heroism must have felt like the entire world was conspiring against him. That is the dark reality of failure—the feeling that the many voices of criticism and ridicule far outweigh the seemingly few voices providing support and love. But Grant's response to this down period in his life was not to quit, give up, or allow the naysayers to win. Not Ulysses S. Grant, not ever. And because he did not allow criticism to defeat him, his fortunes changed with the war. But it was never easy. Failure—and its constant companion fear—would revisit him frequently.

Of course, Grant lead the North to victory and ultimately became the eighteenth president of the United States. However, his presidency was essentially one big scandal after another. But Grant himself was so honest that few historians believe he could have been personally involved. One source notes: "Several of Grant's aides were suspected of inside dealings, but the president himself had been totally fooled."[8] In fact, Republican leaders wanted to nominate Grant for a third term as president, but he refused the honor. Instead, he retired and invested his life savings (one hundred thousand dollars) with his son's banking firm, Grant & Ward. Grant knew nothing about banking, but his son assured him it was the safest investment. Grant was left almost completely destitute when the company failed.

Next, Grant rebounded and struck a highly successful deal with Mark Twain to publish his memoirs. Grant's life was as up-and-down as anyone's can be. He sold kindling on the street and he obtained the Oval Office. He was intimate with both poverty and prosperity. And do you know the most amazing thing about the legacy of Ulysses S. Grant? Although never a people pleaser, he never lost the American people's support. Despite his failures and setbacks, the public considered him a kindred spirit, a man who had fought through the same ordinary struggles they were facing. Yet Grant persevered whether he was peddling wares to strangers on a street corner or shaking hands with the most influential leaders in the world.

The final goal Grant set for his life was to finish his memoirs before he died. Maybe it was his sheer will that he drew upon to complete the task. Maybe it was the encouragement from the people that sustained him. No one knows for sure, but he died shortly after finishing his memoirs. He was a valiant soldier and, like the good soldier he was, he held off death just long enough to complete his assignment, but not before teaching people like me that the reality of life is that failure is inevitable, and so is success through perseverance. Grant's life demonstrates that the question is not *if* you will fail but *when*—and how will you handle it when it happens. As George Bernard Shaw once said, "A life spent making mistakes is not only more honorable, but more useful than a life spent in doing nothing."

———

No one taught me more about coming back from failure than one of my fellow inmates. When I was in prison, my best friend was James Long, a.k.a. Peanut. The nickname is in no way related to a comic strip or a salted nut, and he was anything but peanut-sized. He warmed up with 315 on the bench press and muscles dominated most of his six-foot-four-inch frame. He quickly skipped from childhood to manhood in the inner city of Washington DC and was heavily involved in gang activity. He was convicted of manslaughter after a car accident when, in self-defense, he hit a man carrying a gun with a bat. The man died three days later.

In Federal Corrections Institute–Englewood, Peanut made no apologies for being a Christian. Contrary to popular belief, being a Christian in prison is not vogue nor is it easy. People watch your every move in hopes of screaming "hypocrite" the moment you use a cuss word or explode in anger during an athletic event. The number one question for inmates who become Christians is "why now?" The reasoning goes like this: If you were not going to church when you were not in prison, why go now that you are in prison? This kind of cynicism is not completely unwarranted. Some convicts use Christianity to find protection from "Christian brothers," as they fear being physically abused by non-Christians. Others cloak themselves in the robes of Christianity to gain favor with a judge.

But in Peanut's case, a former gang leader who was physically stronger and tougher than most, no one ever questioned the authenticity of his conversion. Why? Because he had other options. He could have played the role of bully and intimidator, but instead he chose to love people and walk his talk. It is for this reason that he had such an impact on my life and earned the respect of even the toughest inmate critics.

His favorite Bible teacher was Dr. Tony Evans, a pastor out of Dallas, Texas. Every day Peanut would listen to Dr. Evans' daily radio broadcast from the prison-approved Walkman radios that we were allowed to purchase. He even had me listening to the program!

When I was released from prison, I was devastated to learn that Peanut had died in a tragic incident that occurred two days after his release. One of the ways I paid homage to our friendship was by listening to Tony Evans on the radio and reminiscing about the many times we sat in our cell and discussed our lives and futures as we listened to the program. No matter how afraid I was about what my life would be like upon my release from prison, Peanut always believed in me. Although this is not a religious book, I cannot ignore how my faith has influenced my ability to bounce back from failure.

To that end, one day I was listening to Tony Evans and he told a story that was so inspiring it has forever made an impact on my life. This illustration also summarizes the essential theme of this chapter and provides encouragement to those who, like me, so desperately need it. Of course, in the interest of full disclosure, it was given in the context of a sermon, but no matter where you are in that area of your life, you will appreciate the point. One final thing. You must remember the theme music from the popular *Rocky* movie franchise. It's critical to get the power of this story. You know how it goes—*dummm dum dum da dum da da dum* . . . OK, you've got it now.

In the 1990 movie *Rocky 5*, Rocky trains an up-and-coming fighter named Tommy "Machine" Gunn to be a champ. I am willing to bet that you never knew about the deep theological truths that exist in the Rocky movies! Anyway, Rocky is reluctant to train Tommy Gunn (played by Tommy Morrison), but after much persuasion he agrees.

However, after Tommy Gunn wins the championship, he wonders if he could beat Rocky in a fight. Despite his success in the ring, he wants the acclaim he thinks he would receive by beating the one true champion, Rocky Balboa. So the movie concludes not in a boxing ring but with an all-out street brawl between Rocky and Tommy Gunn, which draws a huge crowd of screaming fans—most supporting Tommy.

In one important scene upon which the movie's message hinges, Rocky is losing badly; the action is captured frame by carefully edited frame to show a powerful punch that knocks Rocky out. As Rocky slowly falls to the ground, the viewer can see the background of the people yelling. But as he falls, he flashes back in his memory to Mick, his beloved trainer (played by Burgess Meredith) who had died in *Rocky 3*. Rocky pictures Mick screaming those famous words: "Get up, you bum, get up! Get up, you bum!" The movie fades back to Rocky hitting the ground in front of a huge crowd that now blankets the street. Then there is another flashback. As Rocky lies painfully on the pavement, he again sees Mick shouting from the corner of the ring saying, "Get up, you bum, get up!"

But then Mick adds these key words that make the entire movie: "Get up, you bum, because *Mickey loves ya*." And then things begin to change. First, you hear that music: *dummm dum dum da dum da da dum*. Then, freshly inspired by the memory of Mick's love for him, Rocky gets up off the ground and begins fighting with new vigor. Next, the crowd turns from cheering Tommy Gunn to cheering Rocky Balboa. And with the music playing, the crowd cheering, Rocky gets up and, well, you know the rest—he wins the brawl. All inspired by the remembrance that Mickey loved him.

———

Listen to me, you who have failed. I do not say this as a pastor but as someone who has been laid out on the mat of life more than once, thinking I would never get up. This is what helped me. While I was on that mat, knocked out by wounds that were mostly self-inflicted, I heard a voice. That voice has been heard by millions of people who found themselves in similar positions down through the centuries. The voice shouts with encouragement: "Get up, you bum! Get up! Get up, you bum! *Because Jesus loves you!*" Cue the music: *dummm dum dum da dum da da dum . . .* and I got up, inspired by the reality that no matter how far I had fallen, there was Someone who still had hope for me. Someone who intentionally chose to look at my potential and not my past. Someone who, to this very day, reminds me that no matter who I encounter on the comeback road that may doubt my motives or intentions—and who may even knock me down—He will be there to help me up.

Step Five

EMBRACE THOSE WHO BELIEVE IN YOU!

Remember, George, no man is a failure who has friends.
—FROM THE MOVIE *IT'S A WONDERFUL LIFE* (1946)

If I had to identify the most significant component of coming back from failure, it would be the importance of having people in your life that believe in you, support you, and stand by you. Friends are sometimes the only things that stand between us and a tide of criticism. We may have days, weeks, or even months in which circumstances exceed our own ability to overcome the pain associated with people who question and ridicule our comeback bid.

I call these people who support, encourage, and choose to believe in others despite their past failures *paramedics*. Pastor Chuck Smith illustrates what this paramedic moniker means when he talks about the difference between the police and the paramedics. Who always shows up at the scene of an accident? You'd be right in thinking the police and the paramedics. However, according to Smith, they have two entirely different functions.

The police are there to assess blame. They must make a report of the accident and determine who is at fault. In most cases, the insurance company uses these reports as the primary basis for paying claims. In contrast, the paramedics are there to heal, not to report on who is responsible. Frankly, they could really care less about responsibility, because their primary purpose is to heal those who are hurting *no matter who was at fault.*

On the road to coming back from failure, you will encounter two kinds of people. First are the "police," who arrive with flashing lights and immediately begin assessing the scene for blame. If you have had failures in the past, they will respond even more swiftly. Their role is to be critical of you and your decisions. When they see you heading down a slippery path, your police are quick to conclude that you must be up to your old tricks.

Second are the paramedics, who care little about who was at fault and choose to focus on healing. Some of the best paramedics are people who have failed themselves, because they realize that when a business crashes or a marriage fails or even when personal integrity takes a head-on hit, the person responsible is in need of restoration. They also have vivid memories of how their own police and paramedics responded and how important it was to encounter the latter.

The primary characteristic of a good paramedic is a fundamental, heartfelt belief that people can change. More specifically, the paramedics in your life believe that *you* have committed to change. Based on that principle they become a source of strength to draw upon during the comeback process.

My imagination is simply too limited to explain the value of having a few good paramedics on the scene after the police arrive.

Instead, let me illustrate what happened to me when several "accidents" crowded together in one short week. I was in the middle of a pile up and the "police" were out in force.

———

"My name is Shannon and I admitted myself to this drug rehabilitation center yesterday. I am addicted to painkillers," she mumbled. Most of the people gathered around her in a tight circle stared intently as she continued. "There is a man who pastors a church who has been trying to help me over the past few years. I think I need to see him."

"Who is that pastor?" the group leader asked softly. Shannon hesitated momentarily before answering.

"His name is Barry Minkow and he pastors a church right here in San Diego," she stated. "My mother-in-law has been his personal assistant for almost ten years." When Shannon said that, the man seated next to her who had been otherwise inattentive, suddenly spoke up.

"Hey, isn't that the same Barry Minkow that used to own ZZZZ Best Carpet Cleaning back in the 1980s?"

"It sure is," Shannon replied, nodding affirmatively. "Why, do you attend that church?"

"No. But I've been looking for him for twenty years! I used to work for his company in 1986 and 1987 and my last two paychecks bounced and he owes me thousands of dollars," he exclaimed. "Do you know how I can get ahold of him?" The man was clearly not going to let her continue until she responded. As the rest of the group rolled their eyes, Shannon scribbled my number on a piece of paper.

"Wait 'til I talk to him," the man added as he stuffed the small paper in his front pocket. "He is nothing but a crook!"

"I just think you should stay out of it, Barry," Tony Nevarez advised. In his role as the church's chairman of the elder board, any complaint about me was first filtered through him.

"That's easy for you to say because the accusation and attacks were made about me. I want to know what I am being accused of!" My response was an attempt to goad Tony into telling me what had transpired when a person in the church had accused me of a conflict of interest.

"The accusation was not necessarily just against you. Basically this person has accused the elder board of sweeping issues regarding you and your relationship with the Fraud Discovery Institute under the rug. The person is concerned that you are using church resources like the phones, copy machines, and even secretarial staff for fraud-discovery work. The person also is convinced that FDI is practicing law without a law license."

"You're kidding me, right?" I interrupted.

"I'm not kidding," Tony said gravely.

"So we have someone in the church that believes I am running an illegal fraud-uncovering company, using church personnel, copy machines, and secretarial staff—while simultaneously practicing law? How do I defend myself against that?" I asked naively.

"Good question. I am e-mailing the entire board to make them aware of the accusation," Tony stated. I hung up the phone in disgust.

"I realize you do not know me, Pastor Miller, but I want you to know that if you invest $250 thousand into this deal, you will lose your money," I explained as I weaved through traffic with my wife, Lisa, on the passenger side. She rarely hears fraud-investigation calls, especially both sides of the conversation, so I thought it would be neat to use this call as a way to share that part of my life. We were headed to the church for an evening event when Pastor Miller, an associate pastor at a church in Arizona, had phoned me. I answered the call using my hands-free set, which gave Lisa the opportunity to listen.

"I am only calling you because Gary insisted that I do. Over four years ago a pastor referred Ed Purvis to our church and so far he has an excellent track record of paying people timely returns on their investments." Gary Bruyns had called me weeks earlier because he was concerned that a Ponzi scheme was being perpetrated at his church by Ed Purvis. I was in the process of investigating the investments Purvis was offering several church attendees at more than one church.

I patiently listened while Pastor Miller described the reason for his call. I had done so many of these cases that I could already anticipate what he was going to say before he said it. At this point, he was going to tell me that everyone in the Ed Purvis investments had received their promised 2 percent per month returns over a four-year time period. Never mind that the second wealthiest man in the world, Warren Buffet (who is by far the best at generating large returns to investors over an extended period of time) has only averaged 24 percent annually. Pastor Miller was essentially arguing that this Ed Purvis was in the same ranks as Warren Buffet.

He was also going to tell me that Purvis was a church brother and therefore a fellow Christian of the highest integrity. His decision to invest with Purvis was not based on any objective source,

like audited financial statements, but the many investors who had
been receiving the promised returns over a four-year time period.
I had heard it all before.

"Did you get a chance to read the letter I sent you from the
FBI confirming how many of these kinds of cases I have worked
on and helped shut down in the past?" I posed. My wife smiled
knowingly. Obviously the imputed credibility from the FBI
would most certainly help convince Pastor Miller to consider my
observations.

"All I know is that you are a convicted felon and Purvis has
done nothing wrong," he sneered. Although somewhat predictable, the response was still frustrating. Instinctively I knew this
was not going anywhere so I interrupted.

"But, Pastor Miller, don't you think it is kind of strange that
Mr. Purvis does not allow participants to explain how he gene-
rates these returns and that other investors have no paperwork or
offering memorandum, which is standard for these kinds of
investments? And don't you think it is strange that everyone who
participates in these investments is sworn to secrecy?"

"No, I do not think it is strange at all. The world does business
one way, and we Christians do business by our word," he replied,
as if I was not included in that circle. I felt like reminding him of
the famous statement Ronald Reagan once made in response to
Mikhail Gorbachev. When Gorbachev asked if Reagan trusted
him, Reagan responded, "Of course I do, now cut the cards."

"Look, Pastor Miller. Let me do one thing. Let me Federal
Express you a check from me made payable to any law firm of
your choice that specializes in securities law. Tell that law firm
about the Ed Purvis investment deal and if they say it is legal and

there are no problems—great. It will cost you nothing but a couple of hours of your time. But if they tell you otherwise, which I think they will, then you will save a quarter of a million dollars." I pulled the car into the church driveway and glanced at Lisa who impatiently waited for another snide response.

I made the offer in order to take the "Barry Minkow, ex-convict" problem out of the equation. A neutral law firm of his choice agreeing with my findings would most certainly convince him not to invest, I believed.

"No thanks, Mr. Minkow. You are a felon and Ed Purvis is not."

"But I am also a pastor!" I even tried using my Christian affinity to influence him to at least consider the possibility. *If Ed can do it, so can I!* I thought.

"Yeah, a false pastor who has no business looking into my investments. I know you infiltrated our church with permission from your FBI buddies and you are deceptive and a liar."

"I only lied about being deceptive," I said half jokingly. The car almost shuddered when he slammed down the phone.

By the expression on her face, I could tell that Lisa was in shock. I, on the other hand, had been accustomed to not being believed. The fact that the Fraud Discovery Institute had successfully uncovered similar frauds as confirmed by the FBI mattered little, because—as I had learned the hard way—when it came to credibility, I could not compete with a promised 24 percent annual return! In the fraud-discovery business one learns that people seldom allow things like facts to get in the way of their decision-making process when there is the lure of high-dollar profits. How could I compete?

"He called you a convicted felon!" Lisa was mortified.

"It's been that kind of week," I retorted and squeezed her hand. It was time for church.

———

"You have broken the tax laws, Barry. By not issuing K-1s in 2002 and 2003 to the people who had legitimate write-offs, you are a lawbreaker," the accountant claimed. There was no convincing him otherwise. Simply put, a K-1 is a form given to people who have lost money in an investment so that they can write it off on their taxes.

"Brother, you know I love and respect you, but for the first four years of the Fraud Discovery Institute's existence, we did not even have a checking account because we uncovered fraud for free," I explained, desperately trying to sound benevolent.

"Yeah, but FDI did generate speaking income and book writing income for you," he protested. "How did you record that?"

"On my personal returns. I always pay taxes personally for that income and have recorded it on my personal returns for years. Wanna see them?" I asked. My defense was falling on deaf ears.

"No, I don't, and that still does not justify failing to file K-1s, Barry. You are supposed to be the epitome of financial integrity because you uncover financial fraud and because of your past," he argued. "And you forgot to issue a 1099 in 2001 for $1,000 to a mutual friend of ours," he added. I just listened, thanked him for his concern and hung up the phone.

I sat back and processed the conversation. Technically he was right. I was not exempt from good bookkeeping just because FDI did not have income the first four years of operation or performed work without pay for fraud victims. But a crime? Not when the biggest losers of the benefit of the K-1 were me and my best friend (who had already said he couldn't care less). The week was getting to me.

Eager to move to the next task, I quickly grabbed the phone and dialed my voice mail to check messages. One of them was from the man at the drug rehab center, Chris Borano. After receiving his phone number from Shannon, I had called him to discuss his claim about bounced paychecks. The goal of our conversations was to establish a fair dollar amount to make good on his two bounced paychecks from twenty years ago.

When I first came out of prison, ex-ZZZZ Best employees would occasionally materialize through e-mail or via phone making a similar claim about their last paycheck bouncing. In each case, I made a fair settlement. In this case, I knew Shannon would be made aware of how I handled the situation so I was careful to follow up. But when I listened to my voice mail, all of that changed.

"Look, you jerk!" he said emphatically. "I knew you had not changed. You were just giving me the stall treatment when you asked for my Social Security number and the dates I worked at ZZZZ Best. You are a piece of garbage and a total phony. Meet me here at Sharp Mesa Vista Hospital at 7:00 p.m. tonight if you are not a coward." *Click.*

Something snapped in me when I listened to that message. Maybe it was because I'd learned in prison that if you were called out to a specific place at a specific time and you did not show up, you had to look over your shoulder the rest of your prison life. Or maybe it was the cumulative affect of all these events happening to me in a period of just one week. Not one year, or even one month, but a seven-day time span!

A cursory glance at my watch informed me it was about 6:00 p.m. I mentally repeated the accusations of the week: practicing law without a license, conflicts of interest, doubts and condemnation from people whose life savings I was trying to protect, poor bookkeeping, and, finally, a physical threat. One can only take so much abuse in such a short period of time, I rationalized.

I grabbed my things and darted to my car, determined to physically assault the man who had threatened me. *Law enforcement owes me one mistake*, I thought to myself as I drove to the rehab center. And with that threatening message saved, I could always argue that I felt my life was in danger and that he took the first shot.

I sped off and the phone rang. It was Robert Anglen, a Pulitzer-nominated reporter from the *Arizona Republic*. He was following our work on the Ed Purvis investment fraud case and preparing to write a story breaking the case wide open.

"So why did you offer Pastor Miller 250 thousand dollars to get dirt on Ed Purvis?" he asked.

"I'm not in the mood for jokes," I replied.

"And I'm not joking. I just interviewed Pastor Miller at the church in Arizona and he said you offered him 250 thousand dollars to gather up dirt on Ed Purvis," Robert said.

"And you believe that idiot?" I asked. "Why would I do that?"

"I didn't say I believed him and you can't call a pastor an idiot—can you? Isn't that some kind of sin?" he quipped. Robert was having a little fun at my expense. The problem was context. He was not aware of what I was going through.

"Let me call you back," I said. I hung up the phone, determined to take out my week's worth of rejection, ridicule, and repetitive persecution on Chris Borano.

When I walked into the drug rehab center, my adrenaline was pumping and my heart was racing. My hands became sweaty as I thought back to the last time I got into a fistfight. It was in a kickboxing class (yes, it's true) and I had been pitted against a second-degree black belt. I'd lost—badly. I hoped for better results this time as I marched into the building. What I did not remember in my haste and anger was that I had been at this center before visiting people as "Pastor Barry." I was barreling straight through the reception area when the lady at the front desk recognized me.

"Pastor Barry, good to see you. Who are you here to beat down today?"

Of course, that is not what she said. Instead she asked what patient I was here to love and encourage. I stopped in front of her desk and presented her with a blank stare and a slack jaw.

"He is here to see me," said a gravelly voice from behind me. I instantly recognized that voice from our previous phone conversations and turned slowly to size up my opponent. My stomach tightened and my heart rate increased. The instigator of my outrage was in his mid-forties and a good fifty pounds overweight; there was a large scar on his right knee visible just below his shorts. He was clearly in bad physical shape and I quickly calculated that to my advantage. *This is one fight I could win,* I concluded with a small degree of pleasure. I tightened my fists and remembered how easy it was to break a wrist if I punched him wrong.

I ignored the attendant at the desk and readied myself to

charge at this man who was clearly taken back by the fact that I did not share his apparent physical disadvantages.

The conversation with Tony Nevarez and the accusations of conflicts of interest flashed quickly through my mind. This train of thought continued to my conversation about the Fraud Discovery Institute's K-1 forms and caused me to become even more agitated—as if by then I needed any further prompting. Then the pastor who insulted my concern for his life savings while my wife listened went through my mind. Now there was a reporter who would doubt me because the same pastor I'd tried to help had lied about what I'd said. Finally, I thought about the embarrassment Chris Borano had caused me by calling me out in a public drug rehab meeting and reminding the participants, including someone I was trying to influence, that I had written bad checks twenty years earlier.

I was right. I was justified. I was going to win. Seconds before I was going to act, my cell phone rang. It was my best friend, Tony Jaime.

"Your Steelers are going to suck this year if Big Ben cannot recover from this motorcycle accident," he taunted. "And my Chiefs are going to win it all!"

"This is not a good time," I exhaled through gritted teeth. My tone was unusually serious.

"What do you mean it's not a good time? When I call it's always a good time!" Tony joked.

"No really, this is *not* a good time," I repeated firmly.

Tony had known me for over ten years and had been to hell and back with me. He was a real paramedic who had supported me through the difficulty of an awful divorce and subsequent business debacle in which he personally lost money because of my bad business decisions. Tony knew me better than I knew myself—and I often hated him for it.

"What's going on?" he asked. Silence. "Barry, are you OK?" Silence. "Barry, I need you to talk to me."

I glanced at the man whose nonverbal communication indicated that he was afraid. My eyes flitted to the clerk at the desk who was puzzled by my stare and the fact that I stood motionless talking on the phone. She could sense something was not right. She waved for the security guard to come to her desk.

"I think I need your help," I pleaded. "I am about to go to jail for assault."

"Well, it will carry less time than your fraud," he quipped. I could not help but snicker. "Now sit down somewhere and tell me what's going on." And I did.

I sank down onto a chair in the waiting area and explained to Tony all that had happened that week and why I had come to the rehab center. He listened attentively. The man who had threatened me waited patiently for me to finish the call. I think he was silently rooting for Tony to calm me down.

"Sounds like you had a tough week. Let me just say a few things. First, I want you to know the only reason I personally backed you in that tire venture back in 1999 and later the Fraud Discovery Institute. And that is because if these companies did not work out for any reason, I did not want some outside person who may have invested to ruin your life because they lost their money. I only helped you out to reserve the right to forgive you and not hurt you."

His words sank in slowly. "And as for the K-1 issue, I know I did not get a write-off for my loss, but I did not help you get the Fraud Discovery Institute off the ground to make money. I did it so that you could use your past to help protect people from losing money in the present. And I did that because I believe in you." There was a long pause. I welled up with tears and I turned my head towards the wall to avoid eye contact with anyone.

"Now, go do what you were destined to do for hurting people. You are not a predator—you are a pastor. Now act like one." Tony politely disconnected.

I stood up slowly and wiped my face with the back of my hand. The man gingerly walked over to me.

"I want you to know how sorry I am for shooting my mouth off to you, Pastor Barry," he apologized. "I have a problem with my big mouth."

I thought back to the events of my week that had led me to the point where I was actually ready to resort to fighting an individual in a drug rehab center. That would have been the end of my pastorate as well as my testimony as a Christian. I remembered the many letters I got from inmates in prison who said that my life after prison had given them hope that they too could come back from failure. And I was willing to throw that all away . . . but for a good paramedic.

It was then that I realized that Chris Borano was not calling me out to fight him—he simply wanted someone to care about him. Although I may not have agreed with the methodology he'd used to persuade me to visit, I did know how loneliness and rejection can cloud one's objectivity.

"Would you like to come with me and sit down and talk?" the man requested. "I could use a few prayers."

"So could I," I said with great sincerity.

We sat down to talk and the man explained that he was celebrating his forty-fourth birthday that very day. He had no friends and his mother was the only person who would even talk to him. He told me his story of drug abuse and asked for my guidance. We prayed together and I promised him I would help him acquire a place to live as payback for his twenty-year-old bad paychecks. "I will pay for your first month's rent, your last month's rent, and the security deposit," I said. "And here's fifty dollars for some spending money." After I handed him the money, he gave me a huge hug. I almost cried again. Some tough guy I turned out to be.

I left the rehab center in the driver's seat of my Honda versus the backseat of a squad car.

———

The news bulletin read:

> The southern California office [of the Public Company Accounting Oversight Board] is led by Associate Director of Inspections Gary McCormick, a former partner at Deloitte & Touche and *former president of the Fraud Discovery Institute.* Mr. McCormick began his auditing career in 1980, in the financial services and real estate industries. He spent five years as the Professional Practice Director for the San Diego office of Deloitte & Touche. He graduated from San Diego State University with a Bachelor of Science degree in Business Administration.[1]

"I just want you to know that I think I let you down a few years back," I admitted. I had asked to meet with Gary McCormick at

Seau's restaurant in Mission Valley area of San Diego because I was concerned that I had failed to file the K-1s and at least one 1099 back in 2002 and 2003, while he was the president of the Fraud Discovery Institute.

In 2002, Gary took over as CEO of the Fraud Discovery Institute while I focused on bringing in new business. We became close friends and I even talked him into visiting the church on occasion. But when law enforcement recruiters came knocking in hopes of luring Gary to "the dark side" (my old prison reference to law enforcement), Gary decided to resign as our CEO and take the job as assistant director of inspections for the Public Company Accounting Oversight Board.

However, he was not your stereotypical CPA or law enforcement type of guy. He loved boating, was outgoing and not at all introverted. He was also street-smart as well as book-smart—which made him a very well-rounded fraud investigator. Despite being in law enforcement and excelling at uncovering fraud, he was no policeman. Despite the cynicism that of necessity accompanied his position as assistant director of investigations for the government, he earned his paramedic status. He listened attentively as I explained the situation.

"I already know about this situation because the same guy that told you also told me," he stated while pausing to casually sip his beer. He glanced over my shoulder at the world soccer tournament playing on the screen behind us before making eye contact again. "And frankly I couldn't care less."

His response shocked me at first. "Look, Barry. You are no crook, and I refuse to make the inference that just because a few losses were not filed correctly, you are once again running a Ponzi

scheme. Because that is what this is all about. If you are not perfect in any accounting matter, people—especially us CPAs—will
infer the worst about Barry Minkow and conclude that you are
probably a fraud all over again. Never mind that you expose fraud
and preserve people's life savings. People would rather assume the
worst about you.

"But I am not one of those people. And I have been close
enough to you for extended periods of time to know otherwise
about you—and I am not easily conned. So let it go and keep
doing what you are doing. Now, how are Lisa and the boys doing?"
he concluded.

Just like that he was done talking about the past. We spent
the next hour laughing and remembering the old times when we
would travel the country trying to drum up business for FDI. As
I got up to leave I asked Gary if he would ever consider coming
back and being the CEO of FDI again. He smiled.

"In my mind, Barry, I never left. As far as I am concerned, I
am still the CEO of FDI and I am proud to associate myself
with you."

———

The first thing I learned about Peter Del Greco is that he is a lousy
cop. After all, SEC lawyers are an important part of law enforcement and must maintain that "cop" image at all times. But Peter
Del Greco doesn't—he is much better as a paramedic. I first met
Peter in November of 2003, when he took over the investigation
of my second fraud case, Financial Advisory Consultants out of
Orange County. Despite my past fraud and bad reputation at the
very office he worked at in Los Angeles, Peter cared little about

what I did when I was nineteen years old at ZZZZ Best. He was far more interested in what I was doing with my life now.

It is not easy being friends with a convicted felon when you are in law enforcement, because most law enforcement training hammers home the principle that people do not change. If a man commits a white-collar crime, it is only a matter of time before he commits another one, so look out! This is magnified among SEC employees. Their catchphrase, after prosecuting a particular fraudster, is "See you next time."

But this was not the case for Peter Del Greco. He did not buy into the "people cannot change" system and it was obvious to all who knew him. In fact, in our relationship he went out of his way to make me feel like my past was not an issue for him. When the FDI brought cases that needed affidavits to be filed with the court, Peter would use me—a convicted felon—to sign an affidavit to confirm facts of a fraud case that I knew to be true from our investigation. Peter also never questioned whether or not I was telling him the truth about a case.

The most unbelievable thing Peter Del Greco did was ask me to contact and encourage a lady that he had prosecuted for a fraud years before. He wanted her to come back from her failure, to turn her life around for the better. I have been on both sides of the criminal justice system for almost twenty years and I can say that *I* have never met a government lawyer who would reach out and try to help a perpetrator rebuild her life if there was absolutely nothing in it for him.

This was just one of the reasons I called Peter the day after the drug rehab incident. I explained the accusations that I had encountered and the overall feeling that comes with being on the wrong side of criticism for an extended period of time. Peter, always the good listener, allowed me to finish before he made the following comment.

"There are far more people that believe in you than those who do not believe in you, Barry. It may not seem that way to you, but most certainly in law enforcement circles you have far more people who do believe in you than do not."

The sad reality of criticism is that it often blinds objectivity. You cannot see past it and, as a result, it becomes overwhelming. But people who believe in you pluck you out of the middle of the crisis and allow you to put the problem back into its proper perspective. I thanked Peter for his time, but before I hung up I asked him why he was so willing to believe in me and actually become a paramedic in my life. He responded by saying this about his sister: "I have someone I love very much who, while very young, made some devastating mistakes as the result of bad decisions," he said. "I wanted her to know that I believed that she had the potential for greatness and that I supported her." No big surprise there, he had obviously been a practicing paramedic for years.

I wish there was a way to advertise the need for more paramedics. Although I do not advocate being in perpetual failure, the truth about Barry Minkow is I have a real propensity to fall flat on my face. And because there is no shortage of people who share this propensity, there can never be too many paramedics.

The problem is the job description. Being a paramedic is risky. Believing in people who have failed is a lot tougher than not believing in them. In fact, there is a certain safety in cynicism and skepticism. You are always able to say, "I knew he would fail again, and that is why I did not believe he had changed." But please do not miss this point. This safe but cynical attitude toward those who have failed will work just fine—until *you* fail. Or your son does. Or someone you love and care for fails. Then your view about paramedics will change and you may actually need to become one.

I have learned that on the long comeback road, the most unlikely people have become paramedics. In my case, it was people from law enforcement—the very people who twenty years earlier considered me one of the most dangerous white-collar criminals ever. But as I close this chapter, a few more unlikely heroes from different circumstances are worth noting.

———

Alexander Hamilton's childhood was less than memorable because of his illegitimate birth. He was born in the West Indies on the island of Nevis to a man who was not married to his mother and who abandoned him and his brother. In those days, children born out of wedlock and raised in fatherless homes were an exception to society's norm, and Hamilton suffered severe emotional trauma as a result. It only worsened when his mother died of a fever when he was about thirteen years old. At that time, Hamilton was clearly an outcast in emotional exile with little hope of rescue.

But at age thirteen, when Alexander Hamilton was at the lowest point of his life, two men stepped into the vacuum and decided to play paramedic. The first was a local merchant named Nicholas Cruger. Cruger ran a successful business, and after hearing of Hamilton's tragic upbringing, immediately hired the young man as a clerk. He saw in Hamilton what others did not see. Impressed with Hamilton's natural intelligence and business acumen, Cruger took a huge risk and left the very young Hamilton in charge of his business while he traveled abroad.

The second person who reached out to Hamilton during these early years was Hugh Knox, a new minister on the island. Knox felt a unique burden for Hamilton and took an interest in the orphaned child's life. He opened his library to Hamilton and encouraged him to read; Hamilton was voracious and devoured book after book. Knox also preached to Hamilton on the evils of slavery and the dangers of alcohol abuse.

Two men, Nicholas Cruger and Hugh Knox, were unified for one mission: to encourage, love, and mentor a young illegitimate boy with deep emotional baggage and no apparent future. Their belief in Hamilton would pay off—literally.

In fact, from now on, every time you pick up a ten dollar bill and look at the face of Alexander Hamilton, it should act as a reminder of the power of people who decide to roll the dice and believe in those who are *down, but not out.*

———

Ray Owens loves his older sister Wendy. They are separated by twelve years, which is a fairly significant gap. Wendy married her husband Zac in 1992 and they have four children, ranging in ages from three to twelve. By his own admission, Zac has struggled with an addiction to crystal methamphetamine for over ten years. His addiction materially affected his marriage and his children.

Zac's typical routine would be to stay up all night and play two online computer games, Tribes and EverQuest, while high on crystal meth. Zac became so skilled at these games that he was actually ranked in the top ten in the world. However, he not only used crystal meth to stay up all night, but he also slept through the following day. And he never held down a job for any extended length of time. As a result, Wendy struggled to work and support the family and four children as a cashier at a grocery store. She would try to get Zac to change his ways but to no avail. Ray had also tried more than a dozen times with the same result. Nothing appeared to work with Zac.

One evening things zoomed out of control at home. Despite his drug use, Zac was still a big, powerful, and intimidating man. He actually hit Wendy in the midst of an argument about his failure to retain a job. This was not the first time Zac had become violent, but it was by far the worst.

Wendy called the police and Zac was jailed. That is where most would have written him off, arguing that he got what he had coming! But paramedics don't. They have a way of arriving at an accident scene with amazing swiftness. Out of nowhere, Ray decided to bail Zac out of jail. He then mounted a fundraising mission in order to muster enough money to get Zac admitted to Calvary Ranch Drug Rehabilitation Center in Lakeside, California. Ray visited Zac each day at the center and encouraged his sister to give Zac another chance. Sounds crazy, doesn't it? Ray supported Zac's comeback.

Within thirty days, Zac had successfully completed the program and was released. Ray then helped Zac get a job and rebuild his marriage. Because the paramedic role is contagious, Wendy also decided to be a paramedic for Zac. She forgave him and decided another chance was in order—a chance that Zac did not waste. He immediately got a job, consistently attended twelve-step recovery meetings and, of course, church.

Zac also became a regular visitor at Calvary Ranch to help others who had similar struggles with addiction. Today, almost a year later, Zac is the proud father to his four children as well as a loving husband to Wendy. That is due to the most unlikely of heroes showing up to the scene of his accident—his paramedic brother-in-law, Ray Owens.

———

The fact is, the greatest gift a person can give to someone who is coming back from failure is the gift of believing in him and becoming his paramedic. The reasons for this are obvious. The onslaught of criticism that awaits all who attempt to comeback is enough to rattle the nerves and shatter the confidence of even the toughest people. Sadly, I have seen it happen all too often.

Although I am certainly not the picture of someone who has arrived back from failure, I have made enough strides to *think* I am immune to criticism. But as you can see from reading this chapter, just the opposite is true. That is why I treasure the paramedics in my life. But remember: If there is one thing a paramedic cannot stand, it is having someone he's risked believing in throw in the towel. Trust me, these idealistic risk takers live their lives on the premise that their actions make a difference in the world. So don't prove them wrong by quitting along the way—no matter how tough it gets.

By the way, you didn't think I forgot about that pastor that called me a false pastor and an ex-con and told the reporter from the *Arizona Republic* that I had offered to pay him for "dirt" on Ed Purvis? As it turned out, he did not invest, but he does not give me credit for the advance warning.

The following article from the *Arizona Republic* confirms that FDI's suspicions about this being a fraud were correct—and *they* did give us credit for uncovering another fraud. Of course, you do not think that I invested any time or energy at all by calling this pastor back *after* this story broke and saying something like: "Who's the false pastor now!" or "Next time believe an ex-con when he warns you about a con!"

No, far be it from *me* to do something as shallow and child-like as that, but if you'd like his phone number. . . .

BY ROBERT ANGLEN
THE ARIZONA REPUBLIC

October 6, 2006

Church fund given 10 days to explain itself

State securities regulators are giving owners of a non-profit company 10 days to explain why they should not be shut down, fined and ordered to pay restitution for an investment strategy targeting church members.

The Arizona Corporation Commission alleged in legal filings Wednesday that owners of Nakami Chi Group Ministries International sold bogus securities and misled investors about the scope and size of its assets in order to raise revenue.

"An issue like this is a very serious matter," commission spokeswoman Heather Murphy said Wednesday. "I have never seen our securities division issue one of these (orders) and then reverse itself."

Nakami owners Ed Purvis and Gregg Wolfe could not be reached for comment Wednesday. In earlier letters to The Arizona Republic, Purvis said he was philanthropic and only engaged in private contracts with private parties. He said the state had no jurisdiction in the case.

The commission has been investigating Nakami for more than a year over claims that it was making promises to fund Christian charities while paying investors 24 percent annual returns.

Agents with the Federal Bureau of Investigation confirmed last month that they were investigating whether Nakami functioned as a pyramid scheme, in which funds from new investors are used to pay returns to existing ones without a real revenue source.

FBI officials told The Republic that church members in as many as 10 states had invested several million dollars in Nakami. At least one pastor, church elders and congregation members at Vineyard Church in Avondale and Chandler Christian Church are among those who invested.

"This will be the first domino to fall in this case. And more will follow," said Barry Minkow, a con-man turned pastor who first brought the case to federal authorities and assisted in the investigation.

Minkow, who runs a private investigation agency in San Diego called the Fraud Discovery Institute, said the case is unusual because of the support Nakami has received from churches.

"Despite the federal and state investigations, pastors at churches continued to insist nothing was wrong," he said.

In the filing Wednesday, state regulators outlined two methods Purvis and Wolfe used to encourage investments.

They say Nakami told investors to form "corporations sole," in which investment repayments were made.

The corporations are usually used by churches for holding assets, not for individual investment revenue. Purvis and Wolfe told investors the corporations would reduce their income-tax liability on investment returns, the state said.

Regulators also said Purvis and Wolfe told investors they could put their money into "bridge loans."

"Purvis and Wolfe told . . . investors that the bridge loan investment funded short-term, high-interest loans to small companies," regulators said in the filing.

The notice filed Wednesday gives Purvis and Wolfe 10 days to respond and request a hearing where they will be able to present a defense before an administrative law judge.

Murphy says the hearing strictly deals with state securities violations.

"That does not mean there will not be any other (criminal) charges," she said. "We routinely cooperate with other law enforcement agencies."

In addition to Purvis and Wolfe, the commission accused Phoenix business owner James Keaton of being involved in the effort to defraud investors.

Keaton is the owner of ACI Holdings, where Purvis and Wolfe brought church members who asked for proof of Nakami's holdings.

Keaton has denied that he was involved in Nakami and

said he had no idea that his company was being used as part of Nakami.

Keaton's lawyer said Wednesday that he will challenge the state's case against his client because their accusations are without foundation.

One investor who had dealings with Purvis, Wolfe and Keaton said Wednesday's action by the state was a long time in coming.

"All I've ever been after is the truth," former investor Tony Senarighi of Prescott said. "If you've been doing everything according to Hoyle, then what is the problem?"

Senarighi, who testified before the commission last month, said he and his son-in-law invested more than $150,000 and later got their money back.[2]

Step Six

YOUR BAGGAGE IS THE
KEY TO YOUR COMEBACK

Experience is simply the name we give our mistakes.
—OSCAR WILDE (1854–1900),
playwright, novelist, poet

What possible good can come out of me being a convicted drug dealer?" the inmate asked honestly. He deserved a fair answer.

In the federal prison system, almost 75 percent of the population is in for selling drugs. At the time, I had been recruited by one of the staff teachers at the FCI–Englewood Federal Prison Education Department to guest teach a one-hour class to help inmates who were close to their scheduled release prepare for the outside world. I was initially reluctant because it is very difficult to earn the credibility necessary to be a successful teacher when you are still an inmate! But I gave it a try.

"Well . . ." I answered slowly, trying to buy time so that I could think of something to say in response. "Look at it this way. When you were a drug dealer you did learn the metric system!" Everyone laughed. "But you also learned some key elements about business that can help you succeed when you are released."

"Oh yeah, what are these skills that I learned from dealing a quarter ton of marijuana?" one inmate pressed sarcastically. Now I was in trouble.

"You learned marketing," I responded quickly. Where on earth did that thought come from? "You may have had the wrong product, but you had the right idea. A quality product, competitively priced to qualified buyers is what makes a great marketing strategy. You did just that—which means you have experience and now all you need to do is find a product other than drugs." A circle of faces was staring at me, hanging on each and every syllable. It was one of those moments where I felt as though I was a spectator and someone else was speaking the words issuing from my mouth. But, as we say in public speaking, I decided to go with it.

"And when you sold drugs you made arguments to buyers about the superiority of your product over the competition. You even created an artificial need for your product—which is the approach most Madison Avenue ad agencies take each day. You also learned to keep track of inventory, manage cash flow, and even pay people—albeit for dishonest activities," I continued. I paused for effect as the men listened attentively. "Now, take those skills and apply them to a new product, service, skill, or career where you do not have to look over your shoulder . . . worry about wire taps . . . worry about the competition trying to literally get rid of you. You can make a legitimate living."

———

No matter what the failure, good can be extracted. The fact remains that some positive things can *only* be learned from those of us who have failed, even if you were convicted of dealing drugs or a similar offense. Educators have argued the point for years, but few would deny that people learn best from experience.

Our everyday lives confirm this to be true. Let's say you were getting brain surgery and you had the option of choosing two surgeons. Surgeon A, a former B student in medical school, has successfully performed one thousand brain surgeries before yours. On the other hand, surgeon B, who received straight As in medical school, is a recent graduate and has never performed any of these surgeries. Which doctor would you choose? Of course: the one with the most real-life experience.

Real-life experience, your "failure baggage," can be your competitive advantage on the road to comeback. But sadly, many who have failed do not want to discuss their past out of shame or fear of what others may think, and even go out of their way to hide it. However, this is the wrong approach because people can be significantly impacted in a positive, life-transforming way from our mistakes.

In fact, it is those failures that uniquely qualify us to help others we may encounter. No need to hide the past. It is merely a part of the equation that makes each one of us, well, uniquely us. As the nineteenth-century Scottish writer Samuel Smiles once said, "It is a mistake to suppose that men succeed through success; they much oftener succeed through failures. Precept, study, advice, and example could never have taught them so well as failure has done."

Moreover, and whether we like it or not, our failure baggage follows us like a shadow and is interlinked to who we are because the media and people in general tend to focus more on our failures than on our successes. If there is still doubt as to whether or not this is true, consider the fact that I am still far more well-known for my ZZZZ Best fraud, which had a victim impact of twenty-six million dollars, than I ever will be for uncovering fraud. Yet the dollar amount of the fraud that I have exposed is upward of twenty-five times greater than the victim impact of my crime. (This is not intended to be a self-serving comment—only the reality of my own baggage.)

I cannot begin to count the number of newspaper articles about one of our uncovered fraud cases where the writer mentions in *one line* the fact that I went undercover with the FBI to proactively identify, infiltrate, and help shut down an ongoing financial fraud. Then the writer spends *three lines* describing my past failures regarding the ZZZZ Best fraud and how much money the investors lost as the result of this crime that took place in the 1980s.

Why fight it? Why hide? Why deny the reality that our baggage is part of who we are? That can actually be a good thing. And here is the reason why: if I had not perpetrated the ZZZZ Best fraud, I would not have learned how to identify financial crimes in progress. In fact, the hidden secret I use for successful proactive fraud exposure can be found in my failure.

As the CEO of ZZZZ Best, I lied about how much money the company was earning by saying that my company was performing large restoration jobs on buildings that were damaged by water and fire. By the way, that is all white-collar corporate crime really is—we lie about what we owe and we lie about what we earn. During my tenure at ZZZZ Best, I told investors and Wall Street that we would secure contracts worth millions of dollars from insurance companies by arriving at the scene of a damaged building, extracting the water from the carpeting, deodorizing and sanitizing the affected areas, and replacing the flooring, padding, and anything else that was in need of repair.

This lie gave me the reason to raise new money from investors (there was always another job we were working on to justify our insatiable need to borrow) and it inflated our sales figures, which enabled our stock price increase. So when I went into the fraud-discovery business, I simply used my past baggage to succeed. Here's how I did it.

I examined investment opportunities by asking one simple question: if this company is a fraud, what is the equivalent of a restoration job within its structure? In other words, what scheme or vehicle do the perpetrators use to inflate earnings or conceal what they actually owe? And it is my failure that uniquely qualifies me to perform this task.

The first case I investigated involved MX Factors, a company that claimed to factor receivables for government contractors. Simply put, factoring is when a company is owed a sum of money for selling a product or performing a service but must wait thirty, sixty, or even ninety days to be paid. A factoring company will actually lend money (sometimes up to 90 percent of the amount owed the company) and assume the risk so that the other company can get most of the cash up front instead of waiting. The factoring company will often assume the risk in return for an agreed discount or other services. Since factoring in the MX Factors business model meant borrowing against a receivable, a lien or public UCC-1 filing must have been placed by MX Factors (the lender) on their various customers' accounts receivable in order to secure the loan. I knew that if their business model were true, they would have scores of public filings listing them as the "secured party" on the receivables they were factoring in order to generate the large 12 percent quarterly returns they offered investors. And this, of course, is a public record.

However, when I performed a public record search, there were less than a handful of public record UCC-1 filings listing MX Factors as the secured party. Essentially, this meant they did not have enough customers to justify the returns offered to investors— which in turn meant they were running a Ponzi scheme. This scenario was just like mine years earlier; you borrow from one person to pay off the next. The evidence later proved that this was exactly what they were doing, and indictments and convictions soon followed—but not before they had raised over fifty million dollars from investors.

Here's the point: my past baggage taught me how to think this way. No matter what the failure, there is value to be derived in your baggage because it is a part of who you are . . . minus the fact that you no longer practice the things that caused you to fail.

Now, before you scream "oversimplification," please consider the fact that anyone who has failed in any capacity knows at least one key truth that those who have not yet failed do not know. That truth, which I call the So Much More Is at Stake Principle, allows you to apply the above-mentioned example to any failure comeback scenario.

Admittedly, it may not produce results that benefit society, but it is no less significant. Just as I use my experience to think like a crook to expose fraud, in like manner you can explain how your thought process led to failure by simply explaining the So Much More Is at Stake Principle. A simple explanation of this principle will reveal its value.

If you have experienced a divorce (i.e., marriage failure), think of the time when the relationship first began to deteriorate. In my case, I have vivid memories. My wife at the time, Teresa, had a twin brother who wanted me to officiate his wedding. I had agreed to perform the ceremony, but a few weeks later, I was asked to speak at a large church that televises its services. At the time, my first book, *Clean Sweep,* was out (available now at any garage sale for less than twenty-five cents), and I wanted sales to increase. This would inevitably result from the kind of exposure I'd receive from the church appearance.

Naturally, the speaking engagement fell on the same weekend as my wife's brother's wedding. So, three months before the wedding, I made the decision known that I would be speaking at the church where I would be on television rather than keep my word to Teresa's twin brother (although I did not put it in those terms). I made it sound more spiritual, but the end result was the same.

And here is what I learned by making that wrong selfish choice. There was so much more at stake than a wedding and a speaking gig. What I had actually done was send a message to Teresa's brother—intentionally or not—that he did not matter. I also sent a similar message to Teresa. In choosing to speak at a church instead of performing her brother's wedding, I was telling her that my wants and needs were far more important than her family's or her own.

That action signaled the demise of my marriage, but at the time it seemed like just another daily life decision. And that is the point. We who have failed realize—or should realize—that there is always so much more at stake than what we can see on the surface of the seemingly small decisions we make on a daily basis. My marriage to Teresa did not fail because of some huge fight or unfaithfulness; it failed because of my small selfish decisions that seemed insignificant at the time but turned out to be devastating. Anyone who has failed in a marriage and wants to be honest can point to self-centered decisions as the issue. Remember step one—failure really is all about you (and me). In reality, those decisions sent loud messages to the spouse about the priority of his or her wants and needs in our lives.

The experience of failing is intrinsically valuable because it forces us to hold up a mirror and examine how we got there. In the process of self-examination (which includes the Principle of the Path), no matter what the circumstance, there were a series of small decisions that turned out to be the beginning of the end. Although I still struggle with selfishness and pride, I was determined to learn and apply the So Much More Is at Stake Principle in my current marital relationship. It did not take long for me to get that opportunity.

Lisa's younger sister, Karen, went through an extremely difficult period in her life. She was imprisoned, got pregnant, and really had nowhere to go. So when Lisa indicated that she wanted to reach out to help Karen, I could not say yes fast enough. In fact, Karen has lived with us for almost a year and her life has completely turned around—primarily because of Lisa's love and impact. Had I not been willing to support Lisa's plea to help Karen, this seemingly small decision would have sent a huge message to Lisa about how I view and prioritize the things that are important to her.

Your story of failure has more than one "so much more at stake" component, and that makes your baggage invaluable to others. So don't hide it or run from it. If you failed in business, here is what you know: you know what every convicted white-collar criminal has learned, albeit too late, and that is that your first deviation or criminal act was not very large. No, your first compromise was relatively small. In my case it was the theft of two hundred dollars in money orders.

No multimillion-dollar crime starts out that way. Instead, it begins with small decisions that we made where far more was at stake than we realized at the time. When we share our stories with others, they have impact and meaning that only experience imputes. People need you and your baggage because your baggage is valuable—so do not attempt to hide it under the seat in front of you. Hiding it is not really an option . . . have I mentioned that yet?

For example, who better than Nick Leeson, the man who caused the demise of Barings PLC, a billion-dollar bank in England back in 1995, to tell about the dangers of what is at stake in small decisions? He ended up hiding more than one billion dollars in trading losses, but the first bad trade he hid was only a few thousand dollars. My first crime at ZZZZ Best was not a twenty-six-million dollar stock fraud. And your first compromise was not headline-grabbing news. But it mattered. What we learned through experience is how so much more is at stake than we realize when we make seemingly insignificant bad decisions.

Simply put—those of us who have failed realize the importance of "relied upon." That is, when we make a decision, many people are *relying upon us* and therefore our decisions have far-reaching implications. The thought of facing your children, your employees, or those who love and respect you with the news that you have made a decision that has somehow led to failure is a real deterrent. And it is this deterrent that we who have failed know better than anyone else. So take it from this ex-con: If you want to stay out of prison or avoid failure, when faced with the small, simple temptation to compromise, remember how many people are directly affected and are actually relying on you not to take that path.

———

There is another point about our baggage that has value to others. When we fail, our failures help others who have failed. And, by learning from the failures of others, we can rebuild our own lives. The reason for this is that we tend to lose objectivity when we fail, because we are too close to the wreckage of our lives to be able to provide a solid account of what transpired in the "accident." However, when given the benefit of studying the failures of others, we can identify points of similarity that can be traced from their story to ours. This allows clarity to set in and, I hope, the lesson that will prevent future failure. Imagine that—people who have failed rebuilding their lives off other failures!

Let me share a meaningful illustration of this point from the real-life account of the late John De Lorean. It was from his story that I learned a deep truth about my life that I was too close to discover on my own. Most remember him for the self-named sports car that was at the center of the hit movie *Back to the Future* in the 1980s. De Lorean was indeed a car engineering genius. In fact, while working for General Motors, he was responsible for creating and engineering the Pontiac GTO. In 1981, his De Lorean Motor Company of Ireland began to manufacture cars but soon ran into financial difficulties, which led to his alleged involvement in a massive cocaine distribution deal to rescue the fledgling company's finances.

After De Lorean's arrest in October of 1982, I was well aware of this case; De Lorean was being tried in the Los Angeles Federal Court building and was front-page news for the next eighteen months in my hometown.

On 16 August 1984, he was found not guilty on all counts of drug conspiracy charges. During the time between his arrest in 1982 and his acquittal in 1984, Mr. De Lorean and his then-wife Christina Ferrare, became Christians. That tidbit about their lives became widely publicized. During the trial, he and his wife would each bring Bibles to court with them, a fact that did not easily escape the manipulative mind of Barry Minkow. So when I was indicted in January of 1988, I remembered his acquittal and wanted to follow in his footsteps.

Considering my own inevitable arrest in the late '80s, the first thing I did was become a Christian. Regretfully, I have to concede the fact that one of the reasons I initially became a Christian was in hopes that the sympathy it would generate from potential jurors would be enough to help me be exonerated from the fifty-seven criminal charges I was facing.

Why not, I rationalized, *it worked for John De Lorean.* I even sought out his criminal lawyer, Donald Re. Although others typically receive the credit for saving De Lorean from a criminal conviction, those close to the case rightfully acknowledge that his acquittal was due in large part to the investigative work of Jack and Paul Palladino and the brilliant motion writing of criminal defense lawyer Donald Re.

My goal, as I approached my criminal trial in the summer of 1988, was to follow in De Lorean's footsteps (minus marrying Christina Ferrare, of course!). In fact, when I was in maximum security in the Hole at Terminal Island in early 1988, inmates told me that De Lorean had also spent time there. But something better than an acquittal happened to me during that time—something from his past failures allowed me to see a blind spot in my own life.

You see, the primary witness against De Lorean in the drug conspiracy case was James Hoffman, a paid informant. The government had paid Hoffman to gather evidence against De Lorean in hopes of securing a conviction. In his autobiography, De Lorean recounts that during Hoffman's testimony he became more and more angry at the lies Hoffman was telling about him. He could not believe that this man would make up such stories just because the government was paying him. And then, as De Lorean relates, it hit him.

There at the defense table in a Los Angeles Federal Court room, while the frenzied media looked on and his attorneys fought for his freedom, John De Lorean realized for the first time that looking at James Hoffman was like looking at himself in a mirror—just as Hoffman would stop at nothing, telling lie after lie after lie because he was being paid, so he (De Lorean) also stopped at nothing to make his De Lorean Motor Company successful. And perhaps for the first time, De Lorean saw the type of person he really was through, of all people, the key witness against him in a criminal trial.[1]

By studying this part of De Lorean's life and failures, I learned a lot about the real Barry Minkow. I learned about the Barry

Minkow *that only Barry Minkow really knows* and it helped me identify an area in my life that would aid in my comeback. It took only weeks for me to apply what I had learned from De Lorean's life to my own.

During my criminal trial, one of the government's key witnesses against me was my best friend, Tony Scamardo. I had known Tony since the ninth grade. When ZZZZ Best grew, I gave Tony money and even granted him shares of ZZZZ Best stock. We went out together on weekends, vacationed together, and talked about life . . . which meant girls and the like. But Tony never knew the real story about ZZZZ Best—specifically, that I was a liar and a crook. Instead he attended huge conventions where I was the keynote speaker and heralded as the great entrepreneur of the 1980s. He watched me film television commercials and entertain big-time business people and appear on local television shows.

In his mind, I was a hero. I was the genius business entrepreneur that he looked up to and respected. When the company ultimately failed and Tony found out the truth about me, he was more devastated than even my own mother. But not for the reasons you may think. His devastation was not because I did bad things, but rather because he had heard me say many times that he was my best friend in life and yet I had hid the truth from him about my crimes for over five years.

His conclusion? How could I not share the real truth about my life with the person who was supposedly my best friend? To Tony's credit, when ZZZZ Best collapsed in July of 1987, he continued to be my friend and tried to cheer me up as I waited to be indicted, which happened six months later in January of 1988.

When Tony Scamardo took the stand in my criminal trial in the summer of 1988, he couldn't hide our history. His testimony was devastating because it gave a true picture of me to the jury, one that I did not want them to have. He testified how I was clearly in control of the company and how I enjoyed hanging around the Mafia guys and had voluntarily entered into business with them. He also added that he had never seen these Mafia types threaten me or hit me. Since my defense was "duress"— that is, I did the crimes I was accused of but "the Mafia made me do it"—his testimony contradicted my story of how things transpired.

But I will never forget the day my defense lawyer, David Kenner, asked Tony about an incident that took place near my home immediately following my resignation from ZZZZ Best. I lived in a gated community in Woodland Hills, California, and one day one of the Mafia guys I was doing business with took Tony and me on a walk down the street of my home. This man did not want to talk to me in my home because he feared it was bugged. He knew Tony well, and although this was a private conversation, he had no problem with Tony accompanying us on the walk.

The man then told me, with Tony present, to blame the entire ZZZZ Best fraud on Jack Catain, a former associate of mine who had died of heart failure months earlier. Catain was a known Mafia member and, according to the man I was walking with, a convenient person on which to lay the blame.

This is the type of corroborating testimony that would have given the jury the impression that I was merely following Mafia instructions while running ZZZZ Best. But when David Kenner

asked Tony Scamardo about this walk and the subsequent conversation that ensued about Jack Catain, Tony lied and said the
meeting never took place. Kenner pressed him further and provided specific details of the time of day and location, but Tony
stuck to his claim that the meeting did not take place. I remember sinking in my chair as David Kenner looked at me as if to say,
"Did this really happen and if it did why is Tony lying?" No criminal defense lawyer likes surprises in the middle of a trial and even
though my defense was a lie, the government did not need witnesses to lie to convict me . . . or so I rationalized.

That night in my cell, I thought about Tony's testimony. I
could not believe he had lied while under oath! I was angry. After
all, I had given him money, helped his family financially in a time
of need, and even brought Tony with me on luxurious vacations.
In fact, I'd even let him drive my Ferrari Testarossa, but he fouled
up the transmission, which had cost me close to ten thousand
dollars to repair. *And this is the thanks I get,* I grumbled to myself.

Then I remembered the De Lorean story. Hoffman lied for
the money. De Lorean, in his own words, stopped at nothing to
fulfill his dreams of owning a successful car company. He was
looking at himself in a mirror . . . and so was I. Tony Scamardo
was my very best friend who looked up to me as his hero. The one
thing he'd learned from Barry Minkow was how to lie. How to
boldly proclaim as fact something that he knew to be false when I
and the judge and the jury were looking straight at him. That
night, on a steel bunk bed in my dark lonely cell, surrounded by
cement walls, I realized that the great and everlasting impression
I'd left on my childhood best friend was how to be effectively
deceptive.

I learned that my selfish, deceitful decisions affected *more* than just me. You see, *far more was at stake* when I was lying at ZZZZ Best. More than I ever realized. My decisions were not just witnessed by those I associated with; they internalized and lived by them. If I were going to make it on the road to comeback, I would have to learn that the inevitable result of every close relationship in my life from that moment on would be to leave some kind of lasting legacy, something they had learned as a result of being close to me. The *kind* of legacy I'd leave would now, for the first time ever, matter.

———

It is for these reasons I am convinced that no failure is worth wasting. Sounds so ironic, doesn't it? In their book on leadership, *Leaders: Strategies for Taking Charge,* Warren Bennis and Burt Nanus write about a promising junior executive at IBM who made a mistake that cost the company ten million dollars. He was called into the office of Tom Watson, Sr.—the business legend who founded IBM and led it for forty years. The junior executive was overwhelmed with guilt and fear, to say the least. He walked into Watson's office and blurted, "I know why you brought me in here, so here is my resignation." But Watson said, "You must be joking. I just spent ten million dollars educating you. I can't afford your resignation."[2]

It matters little what the circumstances were that led to your failure baggage. What matters most is how you will use—not hide from—your past. I am convinced that *in the ruins of your failure lie the makings of your comeback.*

The story of Spencer Silver illustrates this fact. He was

working in the 3M research laboratories in 1970 trying to find a strong adhesive. Silver finally developed a new adhesive but, to his chagrin, it was weaker than what the company already manufactured. It stuck to objects, but not permanently. Nonetheless, he didn't discard the formula. It wasn't until four years later that he found a purpose for the adhesive. One Sunday, a colleague of Silver's named Arthur Fry was singing in the church choir. He used slips of paper to mark pages, but they kept falling out of the hymn book. Remembering the weak adhesive, Fry used some to coat the edge of his bookmarks. Success! With the weak adhesive, the slips stayed in place, yet lifted off without damaging the pages. Now the product has found worldwide success, and you can bet I used them to write this book!

Failure caused Spencer Silver to try new things. For me, it was making the transition from the FBI's list of criminals to their list of colleagues. For Chuck Colson, the feared White House "hatchet man" for President Nixon, it was using his subsequent experiences to become the greatest prison reformer of the last one hundred years.

When news of Colson's conversion to Christianity leaked to the press in 1973, the *Boston Globe* reported, "If Mr. Colson can repent of his sins, there just has to be hope for everybody." He started Prison Fellowship Ministries after serving time for the Watergate scandal. This ministry helps hundreds of thousands of inmates and their families around the world.

Still need convincing about the value of your failure baggage? Ever hear of World War II? I am of the opinion that one of the greatest men of the twentieth century was Winston Churchill. The British didn't initially appreciate Churchill and his messages.

During the decades before World War II broke out, he saw Germany's imperialistic intentions and published article after article revealing German military build-up. Churchill urged the British government to build up its own armed forces. But he was dismissed as a "warmonger."

After Churchill's words proved prophetic and the Germans had indeed started the Second World War, Churchill became prime minister. His fearless and decisive leadership inspired the British nation in its darkest hour. Even though Churchill was instrumental in leading the Allies to victory and in defending the British Empire, believe it or not, he was removed as prime minister only two months after the war ended, when his party was voted out of office. A stunning public failure and defeat.

Naturally, he was deeply wounded, but now Churchill suddenly had time to write acclaimed historical biographies, indulge his love of painting, and travel. During his frequent visits abroad, he gave impassioned speeches that only enhanced his reputation as one of the world's most compelling orators. Speeches he never would have given, might I add, had he not failed.

One of his earlier speeches is perhaps the most memorable. On 29 October 1941 Prime Minister Winston Churchill visited Harrow School to hear the traditional songs he had sung there as a youth, as well as to speak to the students. This became one of his most noted speeches, although it is often misquoted. He concluded his speech by stating:

> Never give in. Never give in. Never, never, never, never—in nothing, great or small, large or petty—never give in, except to convictions of honor and good sense. Never yield to force.

Never yield to the apparently *overwhelming might of the enemy*.[3]

Sometimes, especially for those of us who have failed, that "enemy" is your own fear. But by perfecting his skills in speaking and writing, Churchill was once again elected prime minister of England—something he would have never accomplished had he given up in 1945 and not used his failure as a springboard to further hone his talent. Today, Winston Churchill has a reputation as a scholar and a statesman around the globe. More importantly, his life is a testimony of what can be accomplished in, through, and because of failure. He knew all too well that those who are down are not out!

Step Seven

REDEFINE WHAT
A WIN IN LIFE REALLY
LOOKS LIKE

*What will it profit a man if he gains the whole world and
loses his soul?*

—Jesus,
found in Mark 8:36 (NKJV)[1]

The truth about me is I am a very deceptive human being."
These were the powerful and life-changing words of Christian
author Gordon MacDonald as he explained on a radio program
how and why he fell into a life of infidelity. To this day, these
words both haunt and define me because they describe *the Barry
that only Barry knows.* In every area of my life as a former businessman I was deceptive. Whether I was cooking the books to fool the
auditors and Wall Street or secretly borrowing money from the
Mafia, I was a deceptive human being. The man I was is nothing
to be proud of, but areas of vulnerability must be identified on the
road to comeback.

To that end, my biggest area of vulnerability these past years
on the comeback trail has been in how I define the word *success.*

What does success on the road to comeback look like—so that a clear goal is both definable and attainable? In my former life, this was an easy task, as success was tridynamic:

- *Money.* The more I had, the more options were available for me to live for myself and to do what I wanted when I wanted.

- *Power.* I owned the majority shares of ZZZZ Best stock and longed to be in control. The bigger the company was in terms of the number of employees, the greater the sphere of my control.

- *Fame.* From starring in my own television commercials—despite the fact that they were economic disasters—to hiring a full-time PR company, I always wanted the world to know who Barry Minkow was.

However, when my life fell apart, I began to realize that the root cause of my desire to attain money, power, and fame was not an end in itself. No matter what I bought, it eventually got old and lost its appeal. No matter how many times I was written up in some newspaper, within twenty-four hours a new paper signaled the fact I was already old news! The actual reason behind why I defined success the way that I did was much more practical. The truth about Barry Minkow is I am not only a very deceptive human being, but I am also someone who has the propensity to live and invest in only myself. At that point I wasn't quite familiar with diversification, and by that I mean the intentional desire to focus on others. When a business diversifies, it goes into another line of business; like banks going into the financial services industry, for example. In like manner, I believe those of us who have failed must diversify out of a constant preoccupation with ourselves and instead focus on others. In doing so, when we succeed in helping others and are no longer focused on ourselves, we have redefined what a win looks like and potentially leave a legacy in the process.

———

"Lose weight now, ask me how!" That was the popular phrase that launched Mark Reynolds Hughes and his company, Herbalife, on the path to becoming a household name. At age forty-four, Mark Hughes owned 60 percent of the $956 million empire that boasted one million distributors in some fifty countries.[2] That is quite an accomplishment considering most network marketing companies die within the first five years of existence and that he first began selling diet products out of the trunk of his car in 1980.

In 1998 alone he collected just shy of forty-three million dollars in a leveraged buyout of one manufacturer. He owned homes in Beverly Hills, Maui, and Benedict Canyon and had just acquired the biggest house in Malibu for a record-setting price. His choice of attire was a testament to his success: a diamond-encrusted gold ring, a Cartier watch, and custom-cut silk fifteen-hundred dollar suits. Nearing the epicenter of middle age, he could often be found motoring around Los Angeles in his Mercedes or one of his various Rolls Royces. Drive fast and live hard!

He was famous, too, having been written up in many national magazines, including *People,* and was a regular in the society gossip columns. Under Hughes' leadership, the company expanded into international markets such as Germany, France, Spain, New Zealand, Mexico, and Israel, gaining Herbalife worldwide recognition.

However, all of his publicity was not positive. He fought state regulators in California in the mid 1980s and was even hauled before the US Senate to testify about numerous deaths and ill-nesses resulting from Herbalife products. Refusing to be intimi-dated, Hughes mocked the panel after testifying by stating: "If they're such experts in weight loss, why were they so fat?" With all of this pride and success, Mark Hughes must've been the happiest guy at the party, right? After all, he had it all, didn't he? The big house. *Check.* The fast cars. *Check.* The trophy wife (upgrades as well). *Check. Check. Check. Check.*

Yet despite the fame, money, and power that accompany con-trolling a billion-dollar empire, contentment appears to have eluded Hughes. In the *People* magazine profile, his ex-wife stated he was so obsessed with money that he would sit up in bed work-ing out interest rates and finances. "The sad thing is, it didn't seem to make him happy," she noted.[3]

Additionally, according to court records,[4] on 30 November 1996, a Hawthorne police officer pulled Hughes over for driv-ing on the wrong side of the road. The police report indicated that Hughes was making his way from Los Angeles International Airport to the Bare Elegance strip club. A field breath test revealed a blood-alcohol level of 0.22, almost three times the legal limit. After being booked and released, Hughes was charged with driving under the influence and, in April of 1997, he pleaded no contest and agreed to serve three years' probation and pay a fine.

Hughes' life was tragically cut short at age forty-four by an apparent accidental overdose of strong antidepressant drugs mixed with alcohol, in an incident that occurred four years after his arrest for drunk driving. The difficulty is in reconciling these two sides of the man: the brilliant business mind who ran a health food, diet, and vitamin company; and the faltering character who appears to have struggled with alcohol and drug abuse.

My focus is not to write an exhaustive biography on the life and subsequent death of Mark Hughes. He was clearly an accomplished man in many areas and did something that I was never able to do—build a legitimate company. He was never accused of lying about earnings or hiding debt like I was.

Herein lies the dichotomy. On the one hand, Hughes overcame the odds in an industry plagued with failure—multilevel marketing. Few would deny that he was a business success in every sense of the word. In fact, even today, because of the foundation he built, Herbalife still survives and in many areas thrives. At the time I wrote these words (6 July 2006), Herbalife's stock was trading at almost forty dollars a share on the New York Stock Exchange, with a market cap of almost three billion dollars! Mark Hughes lived in a twenty-seven million dollar home and he was in his fourth marriage to yet another model, like the rest. Yet, during one of the company's most successful years, while driving to his twenty-seven million dollar home, Mark Hughes received a DUI on the way back from a strip club.

The unanswerable question is *why?* Why would a man

choose alcohol and a strip club rather than drive to his multi-million dollar home with a beautiful wife waiting for him?

Few are qualified to answer these questions but, regrettably, I am one of the few. Set aside the fact that the points of similarity between Hughes and me border on eerie (minus my felony convictions). Before anyone knew I was a fraud, I, too, roamed the streets of Los Angeles visiting strip clubs and involving myself in other sexually immoral behavior. I was worth over a hundred million dollars, lived in a custom gated home, and the cherry on top was my bright red Ferrari Testarossa. Moreover, I was also secretly addicted to anabolic steroids right in the middle of my sponsorship of a "My Act is Clean, How's Yours?" antidrug campaign in the era of Ronald Reagan's war on drugs!

Although I can only speak for myself, I would say that Hughes bought the same lie I did: It is my right to have my needs met. I have worked for it. I have paid the high price to be where I am and am entitled to get my needs met. *If success means anything it means the ability to gratify needs.* In fact, the reality behind the great appeal of success is the ability to do and get what you want—no matter what it is. Truly successful people, more often than not, get to do what they want to do. The bull's-eye on the target of success is *me!* In a nutshell, success legitimized me living for myself—even if meeting my needs or living for myself contradicted the vehicle by which I earned that freedom to meet my needs in the first place.

Sadly, this is not limited to "success" in the business world, as even a cursory examination of the sports and entertainment worlds reveal similar scenarios of people who, once successful, begin living for themselves no matter who is affected by such decisions. Indeed, the correlation between people attaining success and the subsequent preoccupation with living for themselves is well established.

In fact, just think back to the decisions in your life that you most regret. I am willing to bet that, if you are anything like me, those disappointing decisions all have the common denominator of a choice for "me" over others, the choice of living to gratify *your* needs. Here are some examples of decisions I made for me and my needs.

- The choice to lie and cook the books at ZZZZ Best helped me temporarily because the stock went up. I was labeled the "Wall Street Wonder Boy" but ultimately destroyed the company and 1,400 people lost their jobs.

- The choice to cheat and use anabolic steroids gratified my ego temporarily because of the gain in muscle mass, only to break the heart of my future wife when she learned we could not have kids naturally because I abused steroids.

- The choice to cheat on the woman who loved me back in the ZZZZ Best era gratified my ego at the time, but when the truth came out devastated her emotionally.

- The choice to live a lie and deceive my closest friends and even my parents just so I could control their opinion of me, only to watch my dad agonize every day of my criminal trial as he tried to support the son who forever ruined his name.

The net result of achieving the kind of success that frees us from those things we do not want to do and allows us to make meeting our needs the primary focus of our lives leads to devastation.

REDEFINING SUCCESS

I hate hospital visits. Some people are simply not cut out for them, and I am one of those people. The sad thing is that when you carry the title of "pastor," you'd better be prepared for hospital visits. But that has not stopped me from trying to avoid them. In fact, I even created a "care pastor" job and gave it to Leroy Patton, my long-time friend and fellow church pastor. Despite my efforts at evasion, though, there are still some visits that were unavoidable. Visiting Keith Michael was one of those occasions.

I first met Keith in 1998. Good-looking, well-educated, and a brilliant businessman, Keith decided to walk away from owner-ship in a successful apparel company to take a job as a high school history teacher at Granite Hills High School in San Diego. After the birth of his only daughter, Brittany, he and his wife, Angela, decided the fourteen-hour days that Keith had spent running the company he helped start would prevent him from spending time with their baby.

They timed the market right and bought a nice home in Scripps Ranch, an upper-middle-class suburb of San Diego. In late 1998 they began attending Community Bible Church and everyone instantly loved them. Angela and Keith had it all—great looks, loving hearts, a wonderful home, and a track record of mak-ing responsible decisions for their daughter.

Like most pastors, I try to avoid getting too close to people in the congregation because of what I call the "hot dog dilemma." That is, if you like hot dogs, don't ever watch them being produced at the plant. If you do, you will never want to eat another one! Similarly, if you like me, don't get too close because it is only a matter of time before I reveal my feet of clay, which often leaves people disillusioned. This goes especially for church members, who might have hoped a pastor would not be susceptible to things like selfishness and bad judgment.

I made an exception I will never regret in the case of Keith Michael. He embodied everything I ever wanted to be. He was in great shape naturally and was a real man's man. He surfed regularly, could run for miles (he had incredible endurance), and feared nothing. The most impressive characteristic about Keith was the passion he poured into his students. He was not simply a teacher who regurgitated historical facts; he engaged the students through contemporary illustrations and earned their respect. Other teachers loved him as well. He never missed a day of school for illness and readily gave his sick days away to other teachers.

He never complained about the lifestyle change that he experienced after going from a partner in a successful apparel corporation to the lower, fixed income of a high school history teacher. Angela had the same attitude. She worked as a paralegal for a successful law firm in Solana Beach, and the two of them found their greatest joy in raising Brittany.

Keith and I became close friends after I had broken up with a woman that we both knew. I was devastated by the breakup and wanted to move back to Los Angeles and work as an associate pastor of my former church. The woman I had married when I got out of prison had long since divorced me and remarried. Now the first relationship I attempted after divorce failed miserably, mostly because of my pride, ego, and manipulative actions.

As a result of the breakup, I was emotionally down and Keith saw this as an opportunity to help. He called me daily, took me to sporting events, and invited me to his home for dinner so I would not feel alone. I always tell people in counseling sessions that the sad thing about a breakup is that if you injured yourself physically and, let's say, broke your leg, you would get sympathy because people would see the cast and understand the pain. But internal, after-breakup pain is different. These wounds cannot be seen by the external world, so despite the pain being just as severe as any physical injury—and in some cases more painful—there is little sympathy from those we encounter.

This was not the case with Keith Michael. He encouraged me to not give up or quit my job in San Diego just because of this setback. And then he promised that somehow a special woman would be brought into my life. I did not believe him at the time, but within months after he made the prediction I met Lisa, and the rest is history.

But it was not just me that Keith helped. He would go to Mexico each year and build houses for the poor and homeless. Upon his return, he would share funny stories about his experiences. In one instance, he cut out the space for a window crooked. When the house was completed, it was obvious that this one window looked terrible and really drained the aesthetic value of the home. However, the people were so grateful for the house, they did not complain. Keith was still grateful to have the opportunity to help, but knowing Keith's strength of character, perhaps it is just the rest of us that don't know what "level" really is.

So when I walked into the hospital room that Saturday morning with Tony Nevarez, my boss and chairman of the board of elders at the church, there was immediate familiarity and intimacy due to the amount of history between us.

As Angela tells the story, one morning as Keith was taking off his shirt to shower, she noticed a mole on his back that had a jagged edge and encouraged him to get it checked out. Within days, he had a dermatologist biopsy the mole and the doctor soon delivered the worst possible news: Keith had an aggressive form of melanoma cancer that was advancing quickly throughout his body. His liver was the cancer's first target. Angela had said that Keith only wanted to see Tony and myself to discuss an important matter.

When I saw him, I almost had to stop breathing to keep from crying. He had lost some weight and had various tubes snaking out of his body. His face had lost color and his tray of food sat next to the bed untouched. Tony and I exchanged solemn glances. After the customary greetings, Angela left the room while Tony and I waited patiently for Keith to talk. He cried before speaking.

"I don't mind dying," he declared, "I really don't. I just worry about my fourteen-year-old daughter and wife. I want you guys to take care of them for me." The shock of his statement left us speechless. "I'm going to die," he whispered again.

Keith gravely explained, "There is no cure for the kind of cancer I have. It is like an angry child running through my body and it cannot be stopped." The silence in the room deepened. I thought about this man who did not drink, smoke, or even take an aspirin his whole life. He was previously the picture of health.

Although I would never reveal this in a sermon, the toughest part about being a pastor is facing people stricken with unexplainable terminal illness, especially when they ask the *why me* question. In my opinion, if I were to attempt to answer it, I would be committing a form of malpractice. But strangely, Keith did not ask the *why me* question. Instead, he told Tony and me that he was OK with dying. And then he said something that I will never forget.

"I just wish I could have done more for others in my life," he said. "I feel like such a failure. I wish I could have done more things for more people." I could not help but reflect on all the things that I knew he had done for others and me. If anyone was a picture of unselfishness, it was Keith Michael. Tony and I tried to convince him of this truth by recounting for him various examples of things that he had done for so many people. But he would hear none of it. All he kept saying was, "I wish I could have done more."

I left the hospital that day and drove back to my office, plopped in the chair centered in front of my desk, and tried to process the morning's events. The words *I wish I could have done more things for more people* kept replaying in my mind. It was time I faced up to some things about the Barry that only Barry knew. And I remembered back to an incident that typified the manner in which I lived. . . .

———

I rushed from my office at ZZZZ Best headquarters in Reseda, California, to the softball fields located off Oxnard Street in Tarzana—about a four-mile drive. I had left behind several important meetings, an interview with a stock analyst, and the various tasks that were part of my daily life during my tenure as the CEO of a public company. I thought about the upcoming audit that the accountants were about to perform and wondered if I would still be able to conceal the fraud by creating enough new phony documents.

Then there was the problem of the "burn rate." Between employee payrolls (at the time we had 1,400 employees) and the high interest loans I was repaying to the Mafia and other private investors, I was burning through two million dollars a month.

I tried to suppress the worries of how I would keep pace with servicing these debts while keeping the company running with the appearance of profitability. The softball field was a welcome escape from the tragic reality that was my hidden life as a fraudster. I had accepted the job as the manager of a twelve-year-old girls' softball team in a highly competitive league. I felt immediately tied to the fate of the team since they played at Field 5 in Tarzana, the same place I had grown up playing little league baseball as a child.

Our team was very successful, but not because I was an effective coach; it was because of the fans. Let me explain. Fast-pitch softball was all about who had the better pitcher. At that age, the great pitchers won the duel against the outstanding hitters, so whoever had the best pitcher would usually win.

Now, twelve-year-old girls from other teams may have been able to throw the underhand pitch faster than the girls on my team, but their vulnerability was that they were still preteens. So I hired fans—and lots of them. That's right—I hired fans to fill the bleachers of each of our games and I paid each of them fifty dollars per person per game. But I required a lot of them. Each time the opposing pitcher took the mound, especially if she was good, the fans' job was to yell and scream to distract the pitcher so that the little girl would walk our batters and we would win the game.

I also wanted fans in the stands because I felt that it made me more important. Managing a team that no one comes to watch is no honor, so I managed a team that, at least on one side of the field, had plenty of fans. I'd also spent over thirty thousand dollars to replace the grass and install Dodger dirt in the infield. That was really the only reason the coaches of the other teams and the league president put up with my antics—I knew they needed a new field and I also knew no one but me would lay out the cash to get one. And with the new, well-groomed softball field and the fans filling the bleachers, I felt like my craving to be an important manager had been satisfied . . . that is, as long as we won!

As was my habit, I arrived an hour early to get in some batting practice and infield practice with the girls. As I got out of my car, a man I did not recognize approached me. He did not look happy.

"I do not like what you have done with this league," he grumbled menacingly.

"So join another one—you have to pass ten to get to this one," I replied in my typical condescending tone, as I pulled my glove and clipboard from the passenger side of my Ferrari.

"My daughter is a pitcher on the team you are playing today and what you are doing with these fans to distract her is insane. It's like cheating. Are you some kind of sicko?" he demanded. I was used to ridicule and protests from the parents of opposing teams. But I always mentally justified these complaints with the parents of my girls who loved what I had done for the field and to help the team win.

"Look pal, we put the same amount of people on the field as you do so there is no cheating. And besides, the fans bring an element to the game and a dynamic that will help your daughter be better later," I reasoned. "As long as we win today."

And with that, he drew his fist back and took a swing at my head. My hands were full with a glove and a clipboard and I barely got out of the way as his punch connected, albeit slightly, with my cheek. The man was probably in his late forties or early fifties. He was not in particularly great shape and by the way he telegraphed his punch, it was obvious that pugilism was not his profession.

In contrast, I was twenty-one and on about three different steroids—and it showed. But he was not afraid of me in the least. And it was obvious to me why he was not afraid. He was fighting for his daughter, and the determination he possessed to protect and stand up for her at all costs could be seen in his eyes. People began to crowd around, including girls on both teams. It reminded me of a schoolyard where kids flock to fights like sharks to the smell of blood.

I put my clipboard down but instead of preparing to fight, I actually began to feel sorry for him. Yeah, I would have to fight because my pride was on the line and people were watching. But deep in my heart I could feel a sinking feeling, a dissatisfying dread that up until that day I had never experienced.

During my tenure at ZZZZ Best, I trained myself not to feel. I simply could not afford to begin feeling guilt or feeling bad about the things I had done, because these kinds of feelings would become obstacles to my ultimate goal of success. I had intentionally trained myself to avoid emotion and stay focused on growing the company at all costs, so I could continue living for myself. I had certainly come to enjoy it.

But the feelings were now overwhelming me because this man was fighting for something greater than money or some softball game. He was fighting for someone he loved—even if it meant risking his own safety. And that's when it hit me. What was I fighting for? I had no children playing in the league. In fact, I was not married. I had a girlfriend I lived with but whom I shamefully cheated on regularly. I had parents that loved me, but since both of them worked for ZZZZ Best at that time they were really doing what I told them to do each day. I had high-powered Mafia friends, as long as I kept paying, which reminded me of the two-million-per-month burn rate I had to keep up with. And there I was, in the middle of a softball field parking lot, realizing for the first time in my life that I had no one to fight for because up until that moment, I had only lived for myself.

I was also in a no-win situation. If I beat the guy up, it would be the twenty-one-year-old bully defeating an almost fifty-year-old man. If I lost the fight, I would really look stupid. I was thankful when one of the umpires came over and broke the fight up before anything further happened. After his lecture about being bad examples to the kids, I gathered my belongings and tried to lose myself in the activities of the upcoming game.

But I could not keep the look that was in this man's eyes out of my memory. Even though he had embarrassed me and even thrown a punch at me, I respected him, because he had something to fight for while I had nothing but myself. Unfortunately, it wasn't until the second inning that I remembered. And by then it was too late.

The Mafia family I owed money to actually demanded that I keep a live-in bodyguard with me. He would also follow me in a separate car at all times. They initially told me that it was for my protection, in case other families tried to move in on me, but I knew that it was to watch over me and make sure I did not do something that would hurt their interests. The person they assigned to live with me was Jimmy, a very nice and personable young man—as nice as any bodyguard for the Mob can be. He stayed out of sight most of the time to keep the people at the company from asking questions. He was from Montague, New Jersey, and we got along well, as he rarely did anything that I did not agree with or ask him to do. He was what one Mob boss called "a legitimate tough guy."

In low-risk situations like a softball game, Jimmy would follow about an hour behind me but would always reappear in the crowd of fans in the bleachers. I knew that when he arrived on this day, one of the paid fans that knew who he was would tell him what had happened in the parking lot. Essentially, this meant that the man who initiated the fight with me would be hurt badly. As our team was taking the field in the second inning, I noticed Jimmy's car parked next to mine and darted from the field to the parking lot to find him and tell him not to follow up on the incident.

That is when I saw the ambulance leaving and a small pool of blood in the parking lot. Jimmy had already retaliated against the man who confronted me.

Jimmy noticed the stunned look on my face. "He will be

alright," Jimmy said. "After he sees a dentist." He turned on his heel, walked to the bleachers, and took his usual seat as if nothing had happened.

I stood there alone in the parking lot looking at the pool of blood one more time. Two of the girls called to me from the field. "Barry . . . Barry . . . Barry . . ." But I was lost in thought. My stomach was queasy and I felt light headed. A loving father who only wanted to take up the cause of the daughter he loved had been beaten up, all because I wanted to live for myself and create a fantasy field equipped with imaginary fans that would cheer me on to success . . . a "success" that was nothing more than a veil over the fraud I had become.

———

If coming back from failure means anything, it means learning from past mistakes and not repeating them. Those mistakes are not only limited to the ones that caused the actual failure, but also the ones that established a bull's-eye on the wrong success target. If I have learned anything in the last twenty years, it is that living for myself, while temporarily satisfying, did not make me happy. However, whenever I lived for others, I gained contentment and a feeling of purpose that I never achieved while driving a Ferrari to a strip club or coaching a softball team to a tainted title.

My preoccupation with meeting my needs was, in the past, the greatest appeal of success and the primary reason why I lied, stole, and cheated to achieve it. The problem is, when the money is gone or the terminal illness unexpectedly shows up in a routine physical, even those preoccupied with themselves begin to see the futility of defining success by how well we gratify our needs and desires. As Albert Schweitzer once observed, "I don't know what your destiny will be, but one thing I do know: the only ones among you who will be really happy are those who have sought and found how to serve."

Am I arguing that you should not make money? No. Am I arguing that you should not seek to grow and expand your business or advance your career? Absolutely not. Am I implying that entrepreneurial creativity is evil and true success can only be achieved on a mission field in Africa? Certainly not. But if you are asking these advancements to determine whether or not your life is a success, then you are requiring them to accomplish that for which they were never intended. Believing this does not lower the bar of success on the comeback trail but raises it. Success should be about diversification. You cannot go wrong when the actual bull's-eye on the success target is investing time, effort, and energy in others. If you still have a doubt, allow me to remove it.

———

Rick Reilly of *Sports Illustrated* writes:

> On Tuesday the best man I know will do what he always does on the 21st of the month. He'll sit down and pen a love letter to his best girl. He'll say how much he misses her and loves her and can't wait to see her again. Then he'll fold it once, slide it in a little envelope and walk into his bedroom. He'll go to the stack of love letters sitting there on her pillow, untie the yellow ribbon, place the new one on top and tie the ribbon again. The stack will be 180 letters high then, because Tuesday is 15 years to the day since

Nellie, his beloved wife of 53 years, died. In her memory, he sleeps only on his half of the bed, only on his pillow, only on top of the sheets, never between, with just the old bedspread they shared to keep him warm.[5]

Of course, Reilly is talking about John Wooden. Now, you may be good at what you do, but I doubt you will ever be considered the absolute best of anyone who has ever pursued your profession. You can debate who the best NBA basketball coach of all time may be—Arnold "Red" Auerbach or Phil Jackson—or even the greatest business genius of all time—Lee Iacocca for the way he turned Chrysler around in the 1980s or Bill Gates, the Microsoft billionaire—but there is no debate over who is the all-time greatest college basketball coach. That's John Wooden. He won ten NCAA basketball championships at UCLA, the last in 1975. He won eighty-eight straight games between 30 January 1971 and 17 January 1974, and no one has ever come close to that record.

Even in his nineties, at the time of this writing he is in good health and could easily generate a six figure-speaking fee or a seven-figure book deal advance from any New York publishing house. But he does not. According to author Gary L. Thomas, John Wooden has his eye on another prize: reuniting with Nellie, his wife of 53 years, who died in 1985.[6]

"Every picture on the walls [of his home] are the ones Nellie chose, the ones she wanted up," said John Wooden. "I've changed nothing, except add pictures of the great-grandchildren she never had a chance to see . . . I'm not afraid to die," he says. "Death is my only chance to be with her again."[7]

If anyone had ever really and truly attained success as I defined it (money, power, and fame) it was John Wooden. And yet John Wooden would gladly give up that acclaim for more time with his wife, Nellie, because his true joy in life was derived from relationships that required his time and attention. The irony is that those of us who become preoccupied with success, as defined by money, power, and fame, almost always alienate our family and loved ones in the process because of the sheer hours we dedicate to "being successful." Phrases like "But, honey, I am doing this for you and the kids" or "I do not want our kids to go without because I had to go without" may sound akin to decent justification. In reality, the truth of the matter in my life was that I wanted success for one reason—so I could begin living a life for myself.

I have learned through painful experience that my life in comeback must be based not just on myself and gratifying my wants and needs but primarily on selfless service. The interesting benefit is that if you can radically shift your paradigm, you will end up helping yourself far more by helping others! As author Thomas Wolfe once said, "You have reached the pinnacle of success as soon as you become uninterested in money, compliments, or publicity."

Keith Michael and I still see each other. I do not know how much time he has left. He appears, by all accounts, to be terminal. But after thoroughly helping me deal with my propensity to return to my old ways of defining success and, based on his contention that he, even after all of his selfless actions, "has not done enough," I decided to tell him of his true impact in my life. I wanted him to know that, in the end, everything pales in significance when compared to our selfless investment in others.

Step Eight

TRUTH + TIME = TRUST

The greatest friend of truth is time, her greatest enemy is prejudice, and her constant companion humility.
—CHARLES CALEB COLTON (1780–1832),
English cleric and writer

I t is a simple formula and one that applies to all who have failed. *A lot of truth over a long period of time will restore trust.* I am referring to trust that was compromised during the process of failure. Repairing broken relationships with our friends and family members, and perhaps even our public image, is a process directly connected to the *truth plus time equal trust* equation. The frustration associated with this step is that we cannot circumvent the time element of the process. Like Thomas Paine once said, "Time makes more converts than reason."

Trust is an attribute bestowed upon only those who have proven themselves over time. Despite how committed we are, or how many early successes we may experience in the comeback process, there is really no substitute for a lot of truth over long periods of time. In fact, in the fraud-detection business there is a popular saying: "Time is the enemy of all fraud and the vindicator of all truth."[1]

For those of us who perpetrate fraud, it is not *if* we are going to get caught but *when*—and how many people will get hurt in the process. Time is the unknown variable that subtly exposes our inconsistencies and false promises. I call this the Second Law of Fraudo-Dynamics. You see, the Second Law of Thermodynamics states that things go from order to disorder[2] and, in like manner, over time frauds also go from order to disorder.

The proactive fraud discoverer tries to speed up this process by exposing inconsistencies within the scheme. In contrast, time is the vindicator of all truth, which in the investment community is called *past performance*. We've discussed that Warren Buffet has sustained huge returns over long periods of time (his past performance), which shows not that he's lucky but merely blessed with an incredible skill that's earned him respect in the investment community. Simply put, the *truth plus time equals trust* equation means that consistency verifies authenticity.

However, I have seen far too many people give up on the comeback process because they ran out of patience with the *truth plus time equals trust* equation. Frustrated with their inability to immediately restore trust to pre failure levels among those they love most, these people instead choose to throw in the towel, simultaneously calling foul by hurling accusations like "you really haven't truly forgiven me." But owning our failures also consists of lowering our expectation levels with those we have hurt by allowing them ample time to test our comeback, even as we hedge against disappointment and despair.

The best way to understand the *truth plus time equals trust* equation is to see it in action.

It was 18 September 1984, as thirty-four year old Joe McDermott lowered the shades hanging on the window of his construction trailer in Scripps Ranch, California. Technically the trailer was owned by his employer, Warmington Homes of Costa Mesa, California; but as head project manager it might as well have been Joe's second home. In fact, Joe was a young up-and-comer and one of the most trusted and respected employees companywide.

What the company did not know was that Joe had been in that trailer for three straight days (and nights) on a drug binge that typically consisted of a mixture of cocaine and crystal meth, followed by lots of alcohol to ease coming back down. Closing the shades helped mitigate the feelings of paranoia that accompanied these long drug binges. The worst part of the binge for Joe was when it ended. Although by definition that occurred when the drugs ran out, Joe's end was returning home to reality.

Joe's reality was predictable at this stage of his life. He had rebounded from binges hundreds of times in the past. Typically, his return home consisted of the inevitable confrontation with his wife, Peggy, and his children, Joey Junior and Jessica, after being inexplicably gone for days at a time. Naturally, he thought this time would be the same.

It was approximately 11:00 a.m. when Joe walked into his nearby Scripps Ranch house. The first thing he remembers of that day is seeing a half-eaten birthday cake sitting on the dining room table. Then it hit him: Jessica had turned eight on 17 September and the pile of cake crumbs and frosting was a reminder that he had once again missed a significant event in her life.

The first person who met Joe that day was fourteen-year-old "Little" Joey. He walked up to Joe, who was still reeling from the drugs, and simply stated, "I am ashamed to have you as my father." There was no anger in his voice. It was very mechanical, matter-of-fact, and the words were well-rehearsed. But over the years of drug addiction, Joe had developed a mental filter that blocked negative and insulting comments. Thus, he successfully diluted the emotional pain the words intended to inflict.

But then, out of the corner of his eye, Joe noticed little Jessica slowly approaching him. The motions around him slowed—like the climax of an action movie. Joe knelt down to look at her eye to eye; after all this was his little girl, whom he loved. He loved drugs more, but that did not mean he did not also love Jessica.

"Daddy, please stop these drugs and do not miss anymore of my birthdays," she pleaded with tears in her eyes. He looked at the tears, then at the half-eaten cake directly over her shoulder. Finally, Joe had a moment of clarity—instant clarity. This was unusual because the primary benefit of drugs for Joe was their power to provide consistent emotional numbness. But not this time. In fact, twenty-two years later that moment is still embedded in Joe's mind: the partially consumed cake, the tears, and the simple words. He draws on that experience today when times get tough.

That was the beginning of Joe's road to recovery, because that incident on 18 September 1984 marked the last day Joe McDermott would ever take drugs or use alcohol. That Sunday, with his wife Peggy by his side, Joe attended his first twelve-step meeting at the Good Shepherd Church in Mira Mesa. After the first meeting he felt like an outcast, and he swore he would not return but would instead fight the addiction on his own—but a nice elderly man stopped him before he left. The man's name was Scott Dudley.

From years of experience at these meetings, Dudley could sense that Joe was uncomfortable and uneasy. He approached Joe with arms wide open. After embracing Joe he said, "Kid, it ain't that bad—come back." It sounds simple, but Joe did. For the next twenty-two and a half years, Joe committed himself to these meetings, sometimes attending a meeting every day of the week.

However, as he started doing the steps of the program, he faced *the truth plus time equals trust* component. This came in the form of the mandatory inventory participants must follow, which includes making amends to those who were hurt most by the addictive behavior. Joe followed these steps precisely with his wife, his friends, and his children. But there was a dark secret in his life that prevented him from one last making-amends meeting. It involved his boss, the owner of Warmington Homes.

Jim Warmington had hired Joe twelve years earlier, when Joe was just twenty-two years old. Joe could not have asked for a better boss and friend than Jim Warmington. But Joe had a secret. During the twelve years he had worked for Warmington he had stolen hundreds of thousands of dollars, embezzled from the company to support his drug habit. He had never been caught, but once he committed to a life of sobriety, Joe knew he had to confess what he had done and make restitution. Joe feared this more than anything else—not the restitution so much as facing his boss.

Lest you think this fear came from the possibility of prison, think again. Joe had publicly admitted in twelve-step meetings (long before the statutes of limitations ran out on such an offense) that he had stolen this money from his boss. He knew he needed to confess what he had done and then make restitution but simply could not do it. Everyone, including his sponsor John Maxwell, knew about this secret. Joe had even set aside his entire retirement savings, which at the time had just reached six figures, to cover the amount he'd taken.

But time passed and Joe still struggled with disclosure of the theft to his boss. In every twelve-step meeting Joe attended, he heard a common phrase: "You are only as sick as your darkest secret." Joe's darkest secret was the embezzlement.

For the next several years Joe never missed a birthday party or a family event. Each time he showed up as promised to a ball game, dance recital, school event or, you guessed it, birthday party. Over time, more distance was placed between his past failures and who Joe had become. Peggy, who had by far suffered the most from Joe's past addiction, saw in his decision-making process a man who was putting others above himself for the first time in his life. Even his work became more productive. Within a few years Joe was leading a few twelve-step meetings and even sponsored addicts that he personally helped become and stay sober.

Finally, on a Wednesday in 1998, fourteen years from the time he'd taken his last drug, Joe McDermott decided it was time to tell his boss what he had done.

———

The project managers of Warmington Homes had a name for Jim Warmington's main offices. They affectionately referred to the company headquarters as "Mahogany Row" because of all the expensive dark-wood furniture surrounding the bigwigs. Joe had to drop some paperwork at the main office and swore to himself that if Jim Warmington was there, he would tell him the whole truth. Joe was initially relieved when Warmington's car was not parked in its usual spot but when he entered the office, there he was. Joe explained to him that he needed fifteen minutes of his time and without hesitation Warmington escorted Joe into his plush office.

Joe remembers sitting on a large couch while Jim patiently waited for Joe to do what he had feared doing for fourteen years. As he began to tell the story about the theft and the hundreds of thousands of dollars stolen to support his habit, Warmington would interrupt Joe and say something like, "It's not a problem, Joe. No worries."

But Joe insisted on telling the whole story; his justification for waiting so long was, "I hurt you and your entire family because of my actions and I was embarrassed to come to you because of how good you have been to me for so many years." This time it was Joe, a rugged, tough, hard-working man, who had the tears rolling down his face.

When Joe finished, he reached for his checkbook and wrote a check for hundreds of thousands of dollars, the money that he had stolen from the company. Since fourteen years had passed since he first became sober, he had saved a considerable amount of money in his 401(k) plan. But Warmington said, "I cannot take that from you, Joe." Joe protested and explained again what he had done. Warmington would not hear it.

"The reason I cannot take this money from you is not because

I do not have enough information about what you did," Warmington explained.

"Then why won't you take the money I stole from you?" Joe inquired.

"Because you have shown me more integrity than anyone I have ever met and I will not take your money." He tore up the check and threw it in the nearby trash can. Joe just sat mutely on the sofa. And Jim Warmington wasn't finished.

"I understand you need a liver transplant," Jim said. One of the casualties of Joe's previous lifestyle was his health: he'd contracted hepatitis and severely damaged his liver from alcohol abuse. "I would like to pay for the entire procedure so that you can get a new liver." More tears. Joe was speechless. This was the man to whom he had for years feared to confess what he had done! Joe explained that because he also had diabetes, he was probably not a good candidate for a liver transplant.

When Joe left that day he remembered his daughter's eighth birthday party. Then he remembered how he had restored that huge disaster, not by one big heroic act (something we see in the movies but isn't true for real life), but by keeping his word in the small daily routine of life over a long period of time. He had won the trust of his family back that way and he had now also won the trust of his boss.

Jim Warmington could not pay for a liver transplant because Joe was not eligible for it. Instead, Jim paid for Peggy's breast cancer surgery. Joe never asked, Warmington just found out and wrote the check. Today, Joe has worked for Warmington Homes for twenty-eight years. His boss is still his close friend, and Jessica and Joey could not be more proud of their father. Although his health is still an issue, you would never know it, because he does not complain nor does he allow it to keep him from serving the needs of his family and those who count on him. That is how I met Joe.

You see, for the last ten years, Joe has been one of twenty-two men who meet confidentially in my office at the church. He leads a Christian-based twelve-step program every Wednesday night at 6:30. His small group is by far the most powerful one in our entire church.

——— .

I don't care what your failure is—you could this very moment be drawing the blinds down in your own construction trailer. Or perhaps you are addicted to prescription drugs but feel less guilty because they are prescribed. But you know, and only you know, that you are failing. It could just as easily be a gambling addiction that had been well hidden until your hidden credit card debt came to light, and now your world feels as though it is caving in on you.

Maybe the failure is a violation of a position of trust, or infidelity, or even criminal conduct where the threat of prison looms. How far you have fallen matters little to a man like me whose conduct was so outrageous and evil that it is used as a *don't let this happen to you* story in many college business classes. What does matter is your commitment to comeback, combined with the realization that there is no way to circumvent the *truth plus time equals trust* equation.

In fact, the most difficult of all the consequences of my public failure was *not* prison. Now let that sink in for a minute, because you would think eight Super Bowls in prison (I counted Super Bowls when most counted birthdays) would be the worst part of my experience. But it was not. *The worst part of my experience was the part I prepared for the least . . . dealing with the* truth plus time equals trust *equation.* Let me explain.

When I was released from prison, I had served more time in custody than most white-collar criminals. I had a perfect conduct record for my entire stay, although I'd made some judgment mistakes. But I wrongly assumed that when I returned to freedom, trust and a second chance would be a given for me. This assumption was based on two key factors: serving a long time and being good in prison. *I felt I had already paid my dues.*

Nothing could have been farther from the truth. I made the mistake of overestimating my ability to reenter society and have trust already established based on the high price I'd paid for my crimes and a good conduct record. At the same time, I underestimated the power and reality of the *truth plus time equals trust* equation.

The truth was that people cared little about how good I was in prison or even how much time I had served compared to other white-collar offenders. In fact, as far as they were concerned, my comeback process began upon my release, where the real temptation to revert back to my old behavior existed. Although I disagree with this conclusion, I finally began to understand the reasoning behind it and learned to comply with it.

———

"Barry, Juan Lopez is on line one," my longtime assistant Barbara Brown said from her office. I immediately picked up the phone.

"Did you see yesterday's edition of the *New York Post*?" asked Juan.

"No," I answered. Juan was an old friend and my current partner in the Fraud Discovery Institute. I had first met him when I was at Terminal Island back in 1988.

Juan was the private investigator that my attorney, David Kenner, had retained to be the lead investigator for my defense team. We stayed in touch over the years and when the opportunity presented itself to bring him in as a partner to the Fraud Discovery Institute, I jumped at the chance. Juan was not only a good investigator but also someone who focused on my potential and not my past, even during the dark days when I was incarcerated. If we convicts are one thing, we are loyal to those who believed in us when it was not in fashion.

"Go online and check it out and I'll stop by to see you later," he said.

"Is it a problem?" I asked. I wasn't sure that I wanted an answer.

"No, just something that you need to see." He paused briefly. "By now I would hope that you'd be used to it."

I hung up the phone and quickly logged on to the *New York Post's* Web site. And there it was—in big, bold type:

BY RICHARD WILNER
SUNDAY BUSINESS

August 28, 2005

Rainmaker shoots off a vengeful e-mail

Talk about chutzpah.

The lawyer for the Manhattan investment group accused of defrauding clients to the tune of $3.75 million lashed out at the man who fingered the alleged fraud, telling him the company's executives wouldn't rest until he was behind bars.

"I am going to personally guarantee you that after I am through with you, I am going to send my chauffeur to take you to jail in a brand new Ferrari," Alireza Dilmaghani, counsel to the investment group Rainmaker Managed Living, wrote in the e-mail to Barry Minkow. Minkow, a convicted felon turned fraudbuster, who has fingered more than a dozen frauds in action, alerted the Feds to the Rainmaker case.

Rainmaker raised more than $7 million under the pretense of building assisted-living facilities and returning a guaranteed 25 percent investment return. However, Dilmaghani, 41, and others pocketed $3.75 million, and Rainmaker hadn't purchased any real estate, according to the charges filed by the Securities and Exchange Commission.[3]

———

As in most of the fraud cases we deal with, the Rainmaker case came to my attention from a current investor who'd had second thoughts about his investment. This investor, Josh Kriteman, had seen the *60 Minutes* episode that I discussed in step three and called me to help him recover his investment.

Being threatened by the promoter of a deal that turns out to be illegal was not some new experience for me. In every case I worked on, both the investors and the perpetrators would attempt to debunk my findings or opinion by bringing up my past. The irony is that I was not the one who was the end user of their money! But that fact never stood in the way of their opinion that somehow the ex-con was at it again. Trust me, for a guy who cares too much about what others thought of him, I picked a hard line of work in the fraud-exposure business.

In the case of Josh Kriteman and Rainmaker, we were fortunate enough to be able to recover all of his principal investment (one hundred and ten thousand dollars, which he would later confirm in letter to the US Senate) and shut down a scheme that was growing rapidly in New York and California.

The problem I had with the article was the usual: when would I be remembered for more than my past fraud at ZZZZ Best? After all, the SEC had shut the company down and would not have done so if there was not sufficient evidence, but to the promoter (in this case a lawyer), this minor detail mattered little, as he was going to "personally guarantee" I ended up in prison.

Not long after the Rainmaker case, the 12DailyPro case came to my attention. It was an Internet investment scheme that promised participants huge daily returns in exchange for their visiting certain Web site advertisements. After receiving an e-mail from a concerned family member of an investor, I delved into the company and found it to be nothing more than a Ponzi scheme where new investor money was used to pay back previous investors. You would think the first red flag to investors would have been the promised 12 percent daily returns made by 12DailyPro—but of course not!

12DailyPro was owned and operated by a woman named Charis Johnson. After alerting both the FBI and the SEC and securing evidence for them through FBI-authorized taped phone calls, I submitted a twenty-five-page report documenting my findings. Within days of the report being submitted, Johnson found out about my infiltration of her company and began a campaign to discredit me in several investor chat rooms.

She made sure that the world knew that I was a convicted felon and was secretly being paid by a company committed to her failure. Many people followed suit. Scores of posts brought up my ZZZZ Best fraud, discredited my role as a senior pastor of a church, and proclaimed that "people do not change," so therefore "anything that comes from Barry Minkow cannot be relied upon." Although I should have been prepared, once again I was flattened by the emotional avalanche.

When the SEC formally shut down 12DailyPro and Charis Johnson, confirming my suspicions and findings, the *Wall Street Journal* reported that the company had 300 thousand victim participants and had raised over fifty million dollars. Thinking that I had been vindicated by the evidence, I did something that I should have never done. I revisited the chat rooms and searched for retractions. I looked for the doubters to come forward and apologize. But what I actually found devastated me—even after the *Wall Street Journal* article was published.

"Convicted of a mass fraud in the area of 200 Million dollars which appears to have destroyed many thousands of investors, Barry Minkow was sentenced to 25 years in prison where he served about 8 years. . . . My thoughts on his rehab is this, Once a Alcoholic, for the rest of that persons life they are prone to being a Alcoholic. This teenage criminal committed and was convicted of one of the largest acts of mass fraud in recent history and served only 8 years of his 25 year prison term. Now it appears that man has struck again thru stormpay.com, this time using the SEC and possibly the FBI to hurt many thousands of more people. When do such agencys learn any better? I have heard many individuals state that Barry Minkow is a SCUMBAG and one of the Worst Fraudulent and Corrupted Individuals to Walk This Earth. The folks at stormpay.com seem to think that Barry Minkow is a good honest man, lets look at some information on this so called good and honest man: The Shining White Knight of stormpay.com Barry Minkow."[4]

I should have given the author of the post Peggy McDermott's phone number to rebut the line about alcoholics not changing, but I did not. I just sulked. First Rainmaker and a promise of prison from the promoter, then the public posting on an investment Web site—alleging that I somehow conned the SEC and FBI into believing that this company offering 12 percent daily returns was a fraud. As I read this post, my sons, Robert and Dylan, almost three years old at the time, toddled into my home office.

"What's wrong, Daddy?" Robert asked innocently, noticing the unhappy look on my face. "Are you sad?"

"Daddy is having a bad day . . ." I said, but was interrupted by a ringing phone.

"I get that," Dylan announced. He brought me the cordless phone.

"Barry, it's Sam Antar," the familiar voice said.

"Hi, Sammy," I said affectionately. I dreaded the call because I was not in the state of mind to encourage anyone. I was physically and emotionally drained.

"I just want you to know that I am sending you a hundred

thousand dollars," he said. I heard his words but my mind was slow to process them.

"I'm sorry," I said. *Did he just say what I think he did?*

"I'm sending you one hundred thousand dollars for your institute and I want no repayment; you can do with the money whatever you want."

Wow. I stared at the computer screen where the chat room post stared back at me, daring me to recover from: "Barry Minkow is a SCUMBAG and one of the Worst Fraudulent and Corrupted Individuals to Walk This Earth."

"I don't understand," I stammered. "Why would you do that?"

"Because you are the reason I recovered from my failure in the early 1990s. When I got out of prison for the Crazy Eddie fraud, I read about you and have always looked up to what you have accomplished. And I owe the success I have had over these past years to your example and continuous inspiration." The words on the screen were slowly losing their power over my life as Sammy continued.

"And there is one reason for that. While everyone assumed that it would only be a matter of time before Barry Minkow would once again become a scam artist, you have proven, for over eleven years out of prison, that people can change. That consistency convinced me that I could change and do good . . . and I have." My sons were trying to get my attention.

"Who is it, Daddy?" Robert asked. I paused before answering, as Sammy continued.

"I have done very well in real estate these past years, Barry. My wife and I could not be happier and the good news is—it is all legit. Every dime. I will process the check immediately. Take care my friend." Just like that, he hung up. I closed the window on the chat room and thought about the fact that someone called me out of the blue and just gave me a hundred thousand dollars. Astonishing!

"Who was that, Daddy?" Robert pressed as he woke me out of my daydream. I smiled and picked him up and set him on my lap as Dylan returned the phone to the charger. I looked my son in the eye, probably like Joe had done with Jessica years earlier, and smiled.

"That was God sending someone to remind me that a lot of truth over a long period of time really does equal trust, my dear son. Even when some circumstances would lead you to believe differently."

MARK MAREMONT
WALL STREET JOURNAL

February 27, 2006

SEC Alleges Internet Ponzi Scheme

Freeze of Assets Is Sought After Offer of 44% Return
For Looking at Online Ads

The Securities and Exchange Commission filed a court action seeking to freeze the assets of 12DailyPro, and the agency is accusing the Web site and its operator of running an Internet Ponzi scheme that the SEC said has raised more than $50 million from more than 300,000 investors who were promised huge profits on their money.

The asset-freeze motion, filed late Friday in U.S.

District Court in Los Angeles, seeks to have a receiver appointed to oversee the operations of 12DailyPro and its parent, LifeClicks LLC, according to an attorney familiar with the filing. The Internet company's operator, a Charlotte, N.C., woman named Charis Johnson, has agreed to the proposed order, according to the attorney. The filing wasn't available immediately through the court's electronic documents service.

A judge has yet to rule on the proposed order but judicial approval is considered likely.

Started last spring, 12DailyPro promised "members" that they could earn 44% returns on their money in just 12 days simply by viewing Web advertisements. Thousands of people from all over the world put up membership fees of as much as $6,000 every dozen days. For a while, some got the profits promised. But early this month, 12DailyPro essentially shut down after its primary online-payment processor, StormPay Inc., froze the company's funds, saying it had been alerted that 12DailyPro may have been conducting a fraud.

The SEC said the amount of investor funds voluntarily frozen by StormPay was about $50 million, the attorney familiar with the filing said, although it is unclear whether the full amount is still available. The SEC also is seeking to freeze about $1.9 million of funds transferred from 12DailyPro to bank accounts controlled by Ms. Johnson.

The 12DailyPro site was among the largest of dozens of so-called autosurf Web sites on the Internet. With names such as Auto.ExchangeTrade.com and Vegasurf.com, the sites ride a legitimate trend—the surge in Internet advertising—by promising generous returns to members who agree to view their ads. Most also let members advertise their Web sites to each other.

Autosurf sites can be legitimate, while some promise such huge profits that critics accuse them of running Ponzi schemes. Named for Charles Ponzi, an Italian immigrant to the U.S. who gained notoriety early in the 20th century, a Ponzi scheme is a fraud that promises huge returns to investors but pays them with money from subsequent investors rather than from revenue generated by business.

An attorney for 12DailyPro and Ms. Johnson couldn't be reached for comment. Ms. Johnson released a statement on the 12DailyPro Web site saying her company planned early this week to announce "a compromise" with authorities that "will lead to the resolution of this matter and the beginnings of an accounting and refund process." In the past, Ms. Johnson has maintained that 12DailyPro was a legitimate operation, and she blamed its woes on a commercial dispute with StormPay.

A key figure in the shutdown of 12DailyPro was Barry Minkow, a former carpet-cleaning executive who was convicted of securities fraud in the 1980s before he turned to helping regulators and investigators detect other frauds.

The Federal Bureau of Investigation and various state officials also are investigating 12DailyPro.[5]

Step Nine

YOU ARE GOOD ENOUGH!

He is rich or poor according to what he is, not according to what he has.

—HENRY WARD BEECHER (1813–1887),
American clergyman and social reformer

Michael Lange has been a successful television director for over twenty-three years, having worked behind the scenes of hits like *The Pretender, Beverly Hills 90210,* and, the very popular *OC* television show on FOX. He and I have been friends for over ten years; his children attended a private school where my sister Sheri was the headmaster.

Michael invited me to the set of the *OC* at Raleigh Studios in Manhattan Beach to discuss an upcoming movie project based on my previous book, *Cleaning Up.* He made no apologies for wanting to direct the movie, and this meeting was kind of his way of casting his vision for what would make it on screen if he were chosen to direct.

While we sat in the cafeteria sipping lukewarm cups of coffee, Michael was barraged by associate producers and directors who all wanted "just one minute" of his time. He tried to stay focused on our conversation.

"Barry, there is one theme about your life that I believe reso-
nates with every person who has ever been born," he stated. I
kind of half-listened to Michael but was more interested in what
a studio cafeteria looked like. Cafeterias always reminded me of
prison.

In most federal prisons, inmates are fed three times a day. Each
meal is served in a cafeteria, which means prisoners stand in a long
line, grab a tray and silverware (no steel knives, of course), and
receive food from people whose facial expressions reveal that they
would *never* eat what they are serving up. Then they fill cups with
water or juice and struggle to find a seat in an overcrowded dining area. Surprisingly, Raleigh Studios had a similar feel.

"You were never good enough," Michael declared.

"I'm sorry?" I responded in surprise.

"You never felt that you were good enough. That is the theme
of your life that will resonate with every person that sees your
movie; whoever directs your movie needs to know that theme,"
he said.

I looked directly in his eyes. Suddenly the cafeteria surround-
ings seemed less important. Over an eleven-year time period I had
written two books on my life and never considered the "never
good enough" theme. Sure, I had said in the past that I cared too
much about what others thought about me and how I always tried
to please people rather than do what was right; but I had never
addressed the "why" behind those actions. Michael continued justifying his comment.

"It's right in your book. If it were a snake it would have bitten
you. The very name of your company, ZZZZ Best, gives it away.
Why that name?" he asked rhetorically. "It reveals what you

secretly were struggling with, so you were ZZZZ Best. Because it reveals what was really going on deep inside Barry Minkow when he was an insecure junior at Grover Cleveland High School in Reseda, California. Simply put—you did not feel good enough and thus ZZZZ Best was birthed."

I thought back to Cleveland High School and the feelings I'd had when I attended a sporting event like a basketball or football game. While everyone cheered and clapped for our players, I secretly wished I were an athlete with the whole school rooting for me. But I felt that I was not good enough to make the team. That is when the seeds were planted to somehow create a vehicle, an entity, anything that would put Barry Minkow on the map. It was a defining moment in my life. Michael was right.

"This is the same reason you illegally did anabolic steroids . . . because you did not feel strong enough. The steroids had a heroin effect on you in that it was addicting to have people noticing your size and strength; the compliments made you feel like you were good enough."

It was clear that Michael really knew me. Walking through a crowded shopping mall with a tight muscle shirt and having heads turn fed my insecure ego. It mattered little that I was doing long-term damage to my body, because my feelings of inadequacy far outweighed my future health concerns.

"You even involved yourself with the Mafia and put your life in danger, using your life as collateral for loans because you wanted to build ZZZZ Best into a public company so that you would have national fame. And national fame meant you'd have the accolades of millions of people, which made you, at least while things were good, feel good enough.

"No one with ethics would agree with what you did at ZZZZ Best—but everyone who sees this movie or reads your autobiography will relate to *why you did it*." He paused and leaned closer, as if to tell me something in confidence that should not be overheard.

"And that is because everyone has feelings of not being good enough—even me! Not good enough for a demanding executive producer or show runner. Not being good enough for an exacting mother or father or boss or best friend or even not being good enough for a spouse. We all know and can empathize with why Barry Minkow did what he did, even if we know it was illegal and irrational," Michael reasoned.

I thought back to my first meeting with mobster Jack Catain. I knew I was walking into the lions' den; if I went into business with him (by borrowing money) there would be no turning back. But if I had not borrowed the money that fateful day in 1985, I would not have made payroll and would have eventually gone out of business—which meant no more talk about how the young Barry Minkow was such a successful entrepreneur.

That would prove I was not good enough—which was a reality I was not willing to face. Michael gave me a couple of minutes to ruminate. He knew I was internalizing what he said. He looked over his shoulder to make sure no one was around and took a swig from his water bottle. He saved his best point for last.

"If I did not know any better, Barry, I would even say that your life today is still a pursuit to prove that you are good enough."

"Nonsense," I retorted. I was reacting defensively, not making a logical argument.

"Well, let's lay out the facts. You pastor a church that is growing, have a lovely wife and two children, and uncover sophisticated white-collar crime—sometimes internationally—for law enforcement."

"What's wrong with that?" I asked. "It helps people."

"Of course it does," he agreed. "One or two frauds a year . . . maybe . . . but seventeen cases in less than thirty-six months totaling millions of dollars borders on . . ." he paused for effect, ". . . obsessive! All the while maintaining a full-time job and family—and God knows what else you are doing. Doesn't that strike you as a bit over the top?" he asked, peering down at me.

"Don't get me wrong, these are all great accomplishments that most likely couldn't be duplicated by anyone else. But my question to you, Barry, is, *are you literally killing yourself by burning that candle at every end, day and night, because you still feel that you are not good enough and have something to prove?*'" He asked the one question that my wife, Lisa, had feared asking me in similar conversations.

"I just think you have to unpack the "why" behind what you are doing, my friend. The "what" you are doing is amazing—I just want you to know *why*." Michael placed his hand on my arm affectionately, checked his watch, and indicated that he had to return to the set.

Rarely am I at a loss for words, but this time I could not think of anything to say. I had the long drive back to San Diego to contemplate the why behind the things that I was doing. As I pulled out of the studio's driveway onto the freeway heading southbound, I kept thinking, *I was never good enough—and maybe I still feel I am not good enough.* Over and over.

———

A book called *Emotionally Healthy Spirituality* by Peter Scazzero has impacted my life greatly because he made the connection between people and icebergs.[1] He states that only about 10 percent of an iceberg is visible to the eye. The other 90 percent exists below the surface where our eyes cannot see. And, as in the case of the Titanic, the real danger of the iceberg is below the surface— invisible to the captain or watchman.

In like manner, most of who *we* really are, according to Scazzero, exists below the surface. On the surface, we may portray ourselves to others as confident, reassured, unswerving in our convictions, and even brave. But below the surface of our lives where others cannot see, there exists fear, insecurity, and even feelings of inadequacy, of not being good enough.

As I indicated in step one, fraud is a lot like the iceberg illustration. While I was the CEO of ZZZZ Best, we really did have 1,400 employees, twenty-three locations in three states, and actually performed residential and commercial carpet, furniture, and drapery cleaning on a daily basis. However, below the surface of the company, where no one was allowed to look, we were lying about performing some fifty million dollars' worth of restoration jobs that did not exist. Similarly, Enron Corporation also failed the below-the-surface test. Above the surface they were ranked eighth in *Fortune Magazine*'s Fortune 500 list of top-grossing companies; below the surface they were hiding billions in debt and had created fictitious income.

The real definition of fraud is not the scholarly one found in *Webster's Unabridged Dictionary* but rather a pragmatic one: *fraud is the skin of the truth stuffed with a lie.* Underneath the skin or surface, where people cannot see, lies the real danger. Those of us who have failed and, like me, even tried to conceal what was really below the surface during that failure, must come to grips with our inner fears of inadequacy, whether or not we are lucky enough to have a Michael Lange to point it out for us.

Maybe, like me, perhaps even subconsciously suppressed, you feel that you are not good enough. This feeling of not being good enough may have been, or perhaps still is, the impetus of your failure, because it has leaked into every area and motivation of your life.

There is really only one way to find out what truly lies beneath the surface of your life and if that not-good-enough factor has subconsciously motivated you all the way to failure. This revelation comes by asking one simple, honest question. *Why?*[2]

Why did I feel (and perhaps still do) the need to be "ZZZZ Best" in everything I did? *Why* would I risk my own life and borrow money from the Mafia just to keep an unprofitable company afloat? What was behind the motivation to do seemingly irrational things—all in the name of success? (Or, if you are a philosophy major, it is the causality that I am trying to pinpoint. What was the cause of the motives behind the actions?)

The answer, in my case, was no matter how big my company grew or, for that matter, how big my body grew from illegal steroid use, deep inside I never felt good enough *so I created a life in which I was good enough—even though that life was a lie.* However, I had not yet identified the primary cause or *why* behind those actions and motivations. Before we get to how I eventually did discover the *why* answer behind my zeal to prove I was good enough, let me first bring this point home.

For you, maybe the application is in acknowledging that you learned to believe you were not good enough from your upbringing. Of course, I am no psychologist, but as a senior pastor for almost ten years, I have heard many people explain in counseling sessions that they could never seem to measure up to an over-achieving mother or father. Perhaps your most irrational decisions originate in trying to prove years later that your parents were wrong and you are good enough, as evidenced by your present accomplishments. So the *why* answer (or causality) behind your feelings of not being good enough is your upbringing.

Perhaps it may have been a failed marriage that caused the *not good enough* feelings to dominate your actions. Now you work fourteen hours a day, buy things you do not need, and live life hell-bent on proving to the spouse who left you that you are, in fact, good enough and that he or she was wrong about you. Thus, the *why* answer behind your feelings of inadequacy is your past marriage.

Maybe it was athletics. You knew one day that sports would be your vehicle to stardom (or at least a free college education), so every decision you made fed that goal. But then the reality of high school or college competition set in and it became obvious . . . you were not good enough to compete at that level and you failed. So to compensate for not being good enough athletically, you are now obsessed with making sure your son or daughter *will* be good enough in their sport of choice. This commitment to your child's success has even led to embarrassing encounters with coaches over the issue of your kid's playing time. And the *why* answer behind your feelings of not being good enough is found in dashed hopes and crushed dreams of the athletic achievement that you never experienced.

For me, I cannot blame my loving parents for the daunting presence of not feeling good enough, nor can I pin them on my failure to make the JV basketball team at Grover Cleveland High School in Reseda, California, in the late summer of 1981, nor can I blame my past failed marriage. It was something else and, until I knew for sure, I could not honestly answer Michael Lange's question.

Why was I so obsessed with constantly trying to prove that I am good enough? To answer that question I had to search for the primary cause or event(s) that set in motion my obsession to prove to everyone that I was good enough. So during the long drive on the 5 Freeway from Los Angeles to San Diego, I turned my fraud investigator's skills inward and did not like what I discovered. Remembering that defining moment was like watching a depressing short film.

———

The sign above the snack bar reads Van Nuys/Reseda Little League. Below the sign hangs a banner declaring "Annual Father-Son Little League Game." The camera moves from the banner and focuses on a twelve-year-old boy who takes his lead off second base, while another base runner, a father, takes his lead off third base.

The camera quickly cuts to the scoreboard, which reveals that it is a close game in the last inning, with the team at bat down by two runs, with two on and two out. A voice over the loudspeaker announces, "Up next, Robert Minkow."

The camera reveals a young, ten-year-old Barry Minkow, who shouts encouragement from the dugout to his dad. But his confidence is not shared by the others in the dugout. The camera cuts to a score of faces in the bleachers expressing disappointment that the fate of their beloved team lies in the hands of Robert Minkow. One man in the stands looks to another and says, "Let's hope Robert Minkow can hit better than he provides for his family." In the dugout you can hear the kids harassing young Barry Minkow.

"Great, Barry, your dad is up. This sucks! He can't even hold down a job." Barry turns and attempts to stick up for his father.

"Shut up, jerk—he can hit better than your dad." The boys in the dugout appear to side with the antagonist.

"That don't mean a thing if you drive a beat-up old Dodge Dart and can't afford to keep the heat on in the house," the boy jeers.

Barry lunges at the antagonist. A fight breaks out in the dugout and the parents playing in the game leave their positions and rush into the dugout to stop the fight, interrupting Robert Minkow's at bat.

The antagonist is clearly winning the fight as the scrawny ten-year-old Barry, undersized and underweight for his age, is effortlessly tossed to the ground. Barry wipes the blood running from a cut on his mouth as the parents defuse the situation and jog back to position.

"Looks like you raised a real wimp there, Bob," mumbles

the catcher, who is the father of the antagonist. Robert Minkow says nothing and assumes his place in the batter's box.

"But don't worry. If he can't fight maybe he can inherit the family business to make it," the catcher taunts. The umpire rebukes the catcher with a comment about being a bad example for the kids and play resumes.

Robert Minkow bats left-handed. Before the first pitch, there is an eerie silence in the bleachers. It is in total contrast to the applause and cheering evoked by other players. No one is cheering! This had also been the case for Barry Minkow, who similarly did not receive accolades from the crowd like other players.

———

The fact was that no one cheered. No one encouraged. Not even a *boo* or a *hiss*, which would at least require some kind of emotion. Instead, it was like someone hit the mute button on the stadium. Each person in the stands that day made the decision that they would not root for Robert Minkow or his son. Total silence sent a clear message: total irrelevance. That deafening silence was filed deep into the memory of little Barry Minkow, even though at the time he was unaware.

———

The camera cuts to the two base runners, visibly upset that Robert Minkow is batting. These facts do not go unnoticed by Barry, as we see him in the dugout trying to muster up support for his father. He is ignored.

After taking a strike, Robert rips a line drive in between the first and second baseman. The camera cuts to Barry screaming for his dad's hit and encouraging the runners to score. The crowd stands up with interest but deliberately does not cheer. Again. The runner at third scores easily but the runner at second, the twelve-year-old, stumbles rounding third and is thrown out at the plate. Barry covers his face with his hands. The game is over.

Barry walks by the crowd in the bleachers and hears two men talking. "If Minkow had hit the ball a little deeper that would have never happened." Barry shakes off the comment and surveys the rest of the crowd, hoping to hear just one person compliment his father's hit—or for that matter his own hit during the game. But while many other players receive compliments, Barry is ignored.

"Cassidy Pizza, guys. Let's go," a father says. Several of the nearby players jump up with enthusiasm. Pizza after a game is heaven for kids aged ten to twelve.

"Can we go?" Barry asks the man as his father walks in from the field. The man looks at the boy and sees that his father is out of earshot.

"No," he says flatly. "You guys are not invited." And just like that he is gone.

———

That is how I remembered the incident that day I drove home from Raleigh Studios—like a scene in a bad movie. My father had died in 1996, and just thinking about that event caused me to cry. He and I had never really talked about it. We got home that day and the pain and humiliation was suppressed, because maybe denial could change reality. If I never talked about it and denied it long enough, maybe that afternoon could somehow be undone. But it *did* happen and I never told anyone because I did not want to remember how it made me feel. That was the defining moment that made Barry Minkow *not good enough*.

I quickly took an off-ramp and parked in a Carl's Jr. parking lot in South Orange County. The images from that day were replaying in my head. I kept the car on just to keep the air conditioning running.

"Damn it!" I screamed as I pounded my hands against the steering wheel. Tears were in my eyes. The pain was as real as if I was ten years old all over again. I just kept repeating over and over: "That damn crowd never said a word!" More tears rolled down my cheeks. I slammed my fist against the dashboard.

"If I could get my hands on those people in the stands . . . if I saw them today . . . they would cheer for me now! They would be sorry for the way they treated my dad and me because look at me *now!*" I yelled to myself.

And that is when it all became clear. Crystal clear. I had died emotionally that day at Field 5 of Van Nuys/Reseda Little League in the summer of 1976. A group of people, intentionally or unintentionally, made a permanent impression on me. My father and I were *not good enough* for cheers or applause. For thirty years I had heard that deafening silence subconsciously every day of my life, and it literally drove my every action. If I could somehow get a new crowd to believe I was good enough and they would cheer for me, then the pain would go away—or so I rationalized.

A car pulled in next to me. I tried to wipe my eyes with my

shirt. A young girl, approximately the age I was at that father-son game, followed her mother into the restaurant. I stared at them momentarily. The saddest part of reliving that whole incident was that my father—although he was not perfect or even the best businessman—was one of the kindest, funniest, most easygoing people I have ever met. He never once missed any of his three children's sporting events, even when it meant a career sacrifice.

You might be asking yourself why my father was so disliked. I think it is important to note that he wasn't so much disliked as he was not respected based on the car he drove and the perceived success (or lack thereof) in the business world. Moreover, that year that I played on the A's, I batted last and played three innings per game in right field. My teammates also did not respect the kid who was the worst one on the team. So the cumulative affect of those factors played into my experiences that day.

The very next year when I left the Athletics and began playing for the Braves—which meant different parents and kids— people did accept and like my father and me. But that did not take away the deep emotional pain and trauma of that one awful day. The thought of the pain my dad must have experienced caused a knot in my stomach and my head began to ache.

———

Seventy-one-year-old Leroy Patton was one of the only people I knew who I would not be ashamed to tell what transpired that day. His friendly demeanor made him the most loved person at Community Bible Church. He was one of our staff pastors but, more importantly to me, he was also a close friend. Leroy stands about 5-foot-one-inch tall, is African-American, and has been in ministry most of his life. In the ten years I have known him, he has never judged a person harshly, never failed to love someone even if they had failed miserably, and he always put the needs of others above his own.

I had called ahead and asked Leroy to wait for me at the office. That evening I told him what happened that day at Raleigh Studios and in the Carl's Jr. parking lot where I had the epiphany. I even told him about the father-son baseball game. He listened attentively and waited patiently for me to finish. I cried again. I was glad the offices were empty.

"Barry, I want to tell you a story that will help you deal with this," Leroy said softly. He proceeded to tell me about his five-year-old son Lowell. (Actually, Lowell was five years old in 1970, when the story takes place.) On a Friday afternoon, Lowell came home to Leroy and his wife Linda with the stomach flu. Like any concerned mother, Linda called Dr. Blevins, their pediatrician in Inglewood, and explained the symptoms of her son's condition. Dr. Blevins had been Leroy and Linda's primary pediatrician since Lowell's birth, and was also the doctor for their two younger sons, Leonard and Lawton.

Linda was told to give him Emetrol, or its 1970 equivalent, a liquid medicine that would prevent vomiting. She was told that if the vomiting continued, they should bring Lowell in on Monday.

Later that day, Lowell also had diarrhea but the vomiting had subsided. The next two days were spent trying to get Lowell to drink liquids. But despite the effort of his parents, he only appeared to get worse. On Monday morning Linda and Leroy brought little Lowell to Dr. Blevins's office to be examined. They explained to the doctor that he had severe diarrhea. The doctor checked Lowell out thoroughly, said he was dehydrated, and asked that Linda and Leroy drive him from his office to Children's Hospital for admittance. Leroy remembers asking if Lowell needed an ambulance because he appeared to be weak and listless. Dr. Blevins, in front of his nurse, Linda, and Leroy said, "No, he will be fine without an ambulance. He is just dehydrated. You can drive him over."

They heeded the doctor's advice and drove him to the hospital. But while waiting to be admitted in Children's Hospital, Lowell Patton died. Attempts to revive him failed. An autopsy confirmed that he had died of dehydration. It became apparent that had Dr. Blevins called for an ambulance after examining Lowell, he would have been given fluids immediately by the paramedics and most likely would not have died.

Linda took the death the worst. She blamed herself, despite people's efforts to the contrary. Additionally, their younger son Lawton had to be hospitalized because of the psychological impact of losing his big brother.

"And that is when the phone calls from all the malpractice lawyers began," Leroy explained. "Everyone wanted me to sue Dr. Blevins. And these lawyers promised millions and told me what an airtight case we had and that the doctor's own nurse witnessed the negligence. And they also told me the hospital was liable for dragging its feet in admitting Lowell."

"Did you sue them?" I asked. Leroy smiled.

"Nope, I went back to Dr. Blevins and he could not even look me in the eye. He apologized profusely." Leroy paused. I waited for him to continue. "I forgave him," he said gently.

"Money would not bring my Lowell back to me, and I forgave him. But the reason I forgave him is that years ago, when I was growing up in the South, my momma taught me something that I never forgot. I have even heard you preach it on occasion."

"Oh, yeah? And what was that?" I asked.

"She taught me that people are not valuable because of *what they can do*. They are valuable because of *who they are*—created in the image of God."

He got up from the chair, walked to the door, and called me by the familiar nickname he created just for me.

"And why would I sue a doctor whose value as a person transcends what he did, or in Lowell's case did not do—when God says his value is tied up in who he is!" I nodded my head knowingly.

"Barry, I love you like Peanut loved you. Not based on what you can do—help build a big church that I work at, uncover all these millions of dollars in fraud, speak at conferences. My love for you is based on *who you are*—created in the image of God. Your value is intrinsic and therefore my love for you, and even my love for Dr. Blevins, is unconditional. And when you love people unconditionally, it has a way of taking the pressure off— pressure that you have been living under for far too many years."

His cell phone rang and he picked it up to take the call, but in between rings he wanted to add one more point. "You have made the mistake of thinking that it is the things *you do* that make you 'good enough' in the eyes of those in the crowd at that Little League game, or anywhere else for that matter, when in reality the opinion of your Creator is that you, Barry Minkow, *are already good enough* based on who you are and the fact that—of the six billion people on this earth—there is only one Barry Minkow. And if you do not learn that, Barry, my son Lowell died in vain."

"Hi, this is Leroy," he said to the unknown voice on the other end as he strolled out of the office.

———

You can dismiss this step as the vain ramblings of a pathetic ex-con pastor who is trying to somehow subtly proselytize you, but you would be giving me far too much credit. I want to speak to you in a way that Leroy spoke to me that day. I want you to hear me loud and clear and then test what I am saying with your experience. You are good enough. You are special. You have value and that value is intrinsic and has nothing to do with your career performance, athletic ability (or lack of ability), or past failures—no matter what they are. You are *already* good enough!

Doubt me? Don't even. As you look at these words on this page, just one of your eyes has 107 million cells working harmoniously to enable you to see. You have over 60,000 miles of arteries in your body pumping blood and 9,000 taste buds on the tip of your tongue so you cannot just eat food, but enjoy it. You have 220 bones in your body surrounded by some 600 muscles to protect those bones. And your brain, that's right, the brain you are using this very moment to process and comprehend these words, has 100 thousand billion electrical connections.

In fact, your brain has more electrical connections than all the electrical appliances on the face of the earth. Yet your brain with its 100 thousand billion electrical connections fits in a quart jar and operates, in most cases, for eighty years on ten watts of power fueled largely by cheeseburgers and French fries! Your heart is the size of your fist and weighs less than a half a pound but pumps eighteen-hundred-plus gallons of blood a day, which is enough work in twelve hours to lift sixty-five tons off the ground.[3]

Do you know what these facts prove? They prove that you are specially created and have intrinsic value, *no matter what you can do*. If you are like me, and the impetus of your downward spiral is linked to this insatiable need to prove you are good enough to *whomever*, allow me to once and for all take the pressure off. You are good enough, and if you do not believe this about you, I do! From one failure to another—we have this kinship, I call it the *fellowship of the failures*—you can know that you are good enough!

If you deny this reality and continue in your deep-rooted quest to be good enough, as I have for years, inevitably there will come a time when, if you make it that far, you are no longer on top! Ask any retired athlete who was once the apple of the media's eye but now has deep emotional pain because, that's right, he no longer feels good enough since the media's quit calling. Movie and television stars, models and book authors, CEOs and entrepreneurs, and everyone else who was once at the top of his or her game can tell you the inherent problem in linking performance with *good enough*. Once the performance ceases, the implication is obvious: "You may have once been good enough—but not anymore."

If these people found their personal value in what they could do, in being on top, instead of valuing who they are intrinsically, then they struggled—and perhaps still struggle—with the adjustment of no longer being "ZZZZ Best." And since our experience confirms that no one can sustain being "ZZZZ Best" forever in any field, sport, or discipline, would not the better part of wisdom dictate that it may be wise to reevaluate how we ascribe worth to ourselves—and others?

———

In prison I used to hug men. Now don't get me wrong, it's not what you may be thinking. But when they would come to church or when I greeted them on the weight pile or yard, I would hug many of them. And in medium- to high-security prisons, men hugging men was not the norm. But because I was young, strong, *had more hair*, played tackle football with the guys, lifted weights, and even competed in weight-lifting contests, I was respected. I used this physical respect as leverage to disarm tough gang members and other offenders by hugging them, when appropriate, just so I could let them know that they mattered.

Although I had not yet made the connection to my deep-rooted desire to prove I was good enough, the result of my outreach made the guys I ran into feel a whole lot less evil than they'd been led to believe by those who saw to it that they paid society back for their misdeeds. And do you know what their reaction was to this appropriately displayed affection? Relief. Why? Because maybe, just maybe, and if only for a brief moment, they were not as bad as the prosecutor had made them out to be. And who knows—maybe if they were worth hugging, they were good enough!

Step Ten

BUILD FROM A
NEW FOUNDATION

Only those who dare to fail greatly can ever achieve greatly.
—ROBERT F. KENNEDY (1926–1968),
American statesman

Some years ago on a hot summer day in south Florida, a little boy decided to go for a swim in the old swimming hole behind his house. In a hurry to dive into the cool water, he ran out the back door, leaving behind shoes, socks, and shirt as he went. He flew into the water, not realizing that as he swam toward the middle of the lake, an alligator was swimming toward the shore. His mother—looking out the window of the house—saw the two as they got closer and closer together.

In utter fear, she ran toward the water, yelling to her son as loudly as she could. Hearing her voice, the little boy became alarmed and made a U-turn to swim to his mother. It was too late. Just as he reached her, the alligator reached him. From the dock, the mother grabbed her little boy by the arms as the alligator snatched his legs, which began an incredible tug-of-war. The alligator was much stronger than the mother, but the mother was much too passionate to let go. A farmer happened to drive by, heard her screams, raced from his truck, took aim and shot the alligator.

Remarkably, after weeks and weeks in the hospital, the little boy survived.

His legs were extremely scarred by the alligator's attack. And on his arms were deep scratches where his mother's fingernails dug into his flesh in her effort to hang on to the son she loved. A newspaper reporter who interviewed the boy after the trauma asked if he would show him his scars. The boy lifted his pant legs. And then, with obvious pride, he said to the reporter, "But look at my arms. I have great scars on my arms too. I have them because my mom wouldn't let go."

Max Lucado adds, "You and I can identify with that little boy. We have scars, too, not from an alligator, or anything quite so dramatic, but the scars of a painful past. Some of those scars are unsightly and have caused us deep regret. But some wounds, my friend, are because God has refused to let go. In the midst of your struggle, he has been there holding on to you the entire time.[1]

This story is just one of the many reasons I chose to make God the foundation of my comeback. Just like the old saying, when you find yourself digging yourself deeper and deeper in a hole, the best thing to do is put down the shovel and stop digging. In order for me to do that, I needed a power greater than myself, because I have this propensity to continue to reach for that same old shovel time and again.

But when I became a Christian and began a relationship with God, I brought in a power much greater than any I possess myself as the foundation of my comeback. Yes, I still fail, but this time much of the pain in my life is based on God not letting go of a man curiously addicted to digging himself into deep holes!

In this last chapter, I am not going to preach some sermon or even get "religious" about the personal aspects of my faith. But I do want to share a personal experience that may provide some sound, logical reasons why you, like me, may want to consider making God the foundation of your comeback. If you like things like evidence and debate, you will enjoy this story. But more importantly, if you are anything like me and are also attracted to hole digging, I want you to consider starting a new chapter in your life . . . a chapter that builds from an entirely new (and much stronger) foundation.

———

A few years back, I participated in a debate titled "Does God Exist?" My opponent was Dr. Michael Shermer, the executive director of the Skeptics Society. When a good friend of mine heard that I was debating *the* Michael Shermer, he sent me a "warning" e-mail. Basically, he wanted me to back out of the debate while there was still time—before I was publicly embarrassed by a man who was "a whole lot smarter" than me. Clearly, the author of that e-mail was no paramedic!

To further convince me of the error of my ways by presuming to debate this seasoned veteran, he forwarded Dr. Shermer's latest book, which carried the endorsement of none other than the late Dr. Steven J. Gould of Harvard University, who had written:

"Michael Shermer, as head of one of America's leading skeptic organizations, and as a powerful activist and essayist in the service of this operational form of reason, is an important figure in American public life."[2]

Familiar feelings of inadequacy began to arise as I sat at my desk reading this e-mail. That very moment, the unsinkable Barbara Brown strolled into the office.

"You have to go to that retirement ceremony today," she reminded me. I simply nodded and stared at the computer screen, wondering if there was an honorable way out of a debate that I would clearly lose.

"I know," I answered. Barbara has the keen ability to read my facial expressions.

"You studying for the debate?" she asked. "It's only two weeks away and the tickets are already sold out."

"Don't remind me," I said. "The guy I am debating has a book endorsed by Stephen Gould. I'm going to lose. I cannot believe I agreed to debate on a topic in front of a huge crowd against a guy who knows far more about this subject matter than I do."

"No, he doesn't," she replied.

"What? Are you kidding?" I asked, blinking rapidly.

"No, I am not kidding," she said firmly. "Dr. Shermer may know the formal, scientific reasons behind arguments for God's existence or nonexistence, but you know something that he doesn't know, which gives you the advantage in the debate."

I lifted my eyes from the computer screen and focused on her. Barbara was sitting across from me in the typical seat she occupied when we solved the problems of life together—or at least the problems within Community Bible Church.

"Barry, if God exists, and of course we both share that belief, then any argument that says he does not exist is, well, for lack of a better term, a fraud. And no one knows fraud better than Barry Minkow," Barbara explained. She stood up and circled the chair to face me before leaving.

"So instead of trying to outsmart a clear expert in this field, why not approach the debate from a perspective that only Barry Minkow would know?" she said with a knowing smile. For the first time that day, I smiled too. Barry Minkow knows fraud!

———

Perpetrators of fraud use three techniques to con people. They are not used in any particular order, but where there is fraud, you will inevitably find these three techniques under the rubble of financial loss. I am intimately familiar with these techniques because, much to my shame, I implemented them all—albeit at the time not in some intentional, systematic methodology—to perpetrate the ZZZZ Best fraud. In every case of fraud that I have investigated with law enforcement, these techniques were prevalent. They are as follows:

- Diversion

- Drawing big conclusions from little evidence

- Failure to disclose material facts

Now, before you give up on seeing the tie-in to coming back from failure here, allow me to make the application by illustrating how these techniques were used during my fraud-perpetration days at ZZZZ Best.

To begin with, at ZZZZ Best we *diverted* the auditors, Wall Street analysts, bankers, stockholders, and others away from the fraudulent segment of our business. The restoration jobs we claimed to be performing could not hold up to scrutiny, but the residential and commercial carpet-, furniture-, and drapery-cleaning business could. In the verifiable part of the business we boasted approximately 1,400 employees in twenty-three locations who worked six days a week cleaning carpets, which gave the company an overall appearance of legitimacy.

We also ran television commercials for the legitimate part of the business and even had a carpet-cleaning chemical manufacturing plant for our own private-label carpet-cleaning chemicals. All of the aboveboard enterprises were used to divert the attention away from the restoration business, the part that could not hold up to scrutiny.

The next technique involved the sense of the dramatic for those who questioned the tenability of our restoration business. When we met with big-time stock analysts or Wall Street lawyers before they issued public recommendations on our company, I would make a very simple point using the Yellow Pages. I would regularly draw upon the fraud technique of *big conclusions from little evidence* by instructing these skeptics to immediately open up the Yellow Pages (by the way, if you doubt me, please do this right now so you can see how this technique was used) and turn to the carpet-cleaning company section.

They would comply with the request and would quickly see how almost every carpet cleaning company listed advertised for restoration work on buildings or homes that were damaged by water or fire with bold type stating things like "We specialize in insurance claims." Then I would ask a rhetorical question: "Why are all these companies vying for restoration work from insurance companies? Because it is profitable and plentiful! What gives ZZZZ Best the competitive edge is we have the connections in the insurance industry to secure some of the bigger contracts in this field."

Then, while I had their attention, I would flip to our ZZZZ Best Yellow Pages ad. Of course, we did similar restoration advertising; however, at the top of our ad it read: "Serving this area for over ten years." If they were counting, that meant that I started the company when I was six years old—but I digress.

Did you catch that second technique in action? I used the ad to *draw big conclusions*—the implication that our fifty million dollars in restoration contracts was plausible—*from little evidence*—a simple run-of-the-mill Yellow Pages ad alongside many carpet cleaning companies advertising for restoration business. What I did not tell them is the average restoration job was Mrs. Jones's toilet that overflowed onto the carpeting in her home, not multi-millions of dollars' worth of restoration claims.

This technique was also effective with the media, which is the reason why I always had a public relations firm on a monthly retainer for ZZZZ Best. The more positive publicity I received from newspapers, magazines, and television shows, the more I was able to imply that ZZZZ Best was legitimate.

When I appeared on the *Oprah Winfrey Show* in 1987 and boasted of the company's success, the impression to the viewing public was that I had to be telling the truth about ZZZZ Best's financial condition; otherwise Oprah would not have had me on the show. This is no potshot at Oprah, who had no clue that I was a liar and a thief. But by being on her show I caused the public to *draw a big conclusion*: I was the CEO of a hugely successful public company—*from little evidence*—an appearance on a television show.

Another use of this technique is worth noting. I actually set up a scene, Hollywood-style, of a restoration job in progress, took a picture of it, and placed that picture on the prospectus of our investor offering. We hoped the potential investor would draw the big conclusion—all fifty million dollars in restoration work we were claiming to be performing was legitimate—based on the evidence of a single picture.

We also *failed to disclose material facts*. For example, I never disclosed the fact that I was secretly borrowing money from the Mafia and siphoning from ZZZZ Best to make the usurious payments on these loans. The auditors probably would have wanted to know such material facts before signing a clean opinion.

On one occasion, a lawyer for one of the investment banking firms from which we were raising money identified a public filing in which I had been sued by Jack Catain in 1985. The lawyer quickly concluded that I had concealed my relationship with a known mobster (who at the time was under federal indictment) from him and his client.

I explained that the suit was bogus and that the US Attorney's office in Los Angeles actually viewed me as a victim of Catain. Of course, in context, the US Attorney's office was not aware that I was a willing participant with Catain and that his suit was more a falling-out among thieves than anything else. However, at the time the government's position was that my youth and inexperience allowed me to be victimized by the more seasoned Jack Catain. The US Attorney explained this to the inquisitive lawyer and the issue was immediately dropped. Sadly, only some sixty days later I was able to raise about eighteen million dollars from Wall Street.

At the time, what I feared would happen was that the investment banking firm or their lawyer would say, "Hey, if Minkow concealed this material fact—namely that he had a past relationship with Jack Catain, an indicted mobster—what other material facts is he withholding?" The reason for that important question is that fraud, by definition, is *the failure to disclose material facts* and to actively, through lies and deception, keep those facts from ever being disclosed or discovered by anyone investigating. But no one ever asked the what-else-must-he-be-hiding question.

I know what you are thinking: what do this education in the three fraud techniques and a debate on the existence of God have to do with step ten, building a new foundation? The answer is simple. I am convinced that in order to come back from failure, you and I need someone greater than either of us as the foundation for that comeback. I make no apologies for stating that the "someone" in my life is God.

I am also convinced that if you reject the concept of God or his existence, you may have been *conned* into that current view. If that is actually the case, who better than me to detect it—as Barbara Brown so sagely advised.

Admittedly, you have not been conned out of your money, but you have been conned out of something I believe is far more valuable . . . and therefore it's worth addressing. The irony is this con has been perpetrated through the use of the same three fraud techniques that I and others have used in the investment fraud arena. In fact, the parallels are uncanny. This reality first came to my attention when I prepared for the debate against Michael Shermer.

Let me state up front that I will not digress into a sermon or an endless citation of quotes to establish my point. Rather, I will use the three simple arguments I used in my debate with Dr. Shermer to show why belief in God is a plausible, rational view, and how arguments to the contrary appear to employ diversion, draw big conclusions from little evidence, and fail to disclose material facts. Although I am talking about the traditional Judeo-Christian God, you need to *trust me* that this will be a unique and fun way to look at this subject, as I bet you never heard a fraud investigator's approach to this particular topic. You may be leery of an ex-con saying *trust me,* but work with me here. . . .

I mean no disrespect to those who may disagree with my approach or conclusions but only ask that my three arguments be viewed with an open mind. I hope that I will be able to provide a positive rationale for giving God a chance to be at the very foundation of your comeback. It beats the heck out of a shovel!

The sold-out crowd slowly filed into the meeting room at the Marriott Hotel where the debate was being held. I found Michael Shermer in the lobby, where he was nursing what was left of his first drink. He was calm and collected—in sharp contrast to me, despite my efforts. He casually asked the waitress for another drink, and made some joke about pastors not drinking when I ordered a Diet Coke. After exchanging pleasantries, we talked.

He explained that he had grown up a Christian and by the time he was in college he actually majored in theology at Pepperdine University. But he soon became disillusioned with Christianity and realized that "science, especially the theory of evolution, disproved any sort of special creator."[3]

"And you did not want to have to turn your brain off in the lobby of the church before coming into the sanctuary anymore?" I asked.

"Exactly," he said, surprised that I actually summed up his feelings in that type of analogy. "Christianity is based solely on blind faith, not evidence and reason."

"So if I understand you correctly, it is reasonable to believe in evolution and unreasonable to believe that God exists?" I asked.

"Absolutely," he responded. "And, of course, I cannot prove God does not exist any more than I can disprove that there is not an invisible elf sitting on the top of your head right now—but I think that it is highly likely, based on scientific evidence, that neither exist."

"God or the elf?" I asked, trying to be funny. He was not amused.

"Neither," he retorted.

And herein lies the problem. The impression given—from the college class on cosmology to the television network Comedy Central—is that it is an intellectual joke to naively believe that God exists in the face of so much scientific evidence that appears to prove otherwise. Thus, God's existence is the intellectual equivalent of an invisible elf resting on my head. And no person coming back from failure wants to place the foundation for his or her comeback on the intellectual equivalent of an invisible elf!

———

You only need to know one thing to determine financial fraud, and it's this: Every fraud has a "restoration job"! If an investment is a fraud, and fraud is defined loosely as *lying about earnings* and *lying about what is owed,* then there is a vehicle (such as ZZZZ Best's restoration jobs) being used by the perpetrator to inflate sales and hide debt. The secret to proactive fraud-discovery is finding the equivalent of that restoration job in a particular investment.

To do that, one must implement what I call the normally-and-regularly test. Let's say the investment deal is a clothes-hanger company offering investors a 40 percent annual return on their money. The first question a proactive fraud seeker needs to ask is if clothes-hanger companies *normally and regularly* achieve returns of 40 percent or more. I say "more" because 40 percent is what the investors are being offered and the company still needs to make a profit; so in actuality the number is even higher than 40 percent.

However, if a study of the clothes-hanger industry reveals that the nation's best-run hanger companies only generate, on average, returns of 15 percent annually, you have a red flag for fraud. Why? Because it fails the normally-and-regularly test. Normally and regularly, companies in the clothes-hanger business only earn 15 percent a year, not 40 percent, and that is a cause for concern.[4]

In like manner, there is a principle in science called the principle of uniformity (or analogy) that I used in the debate with Dr. Shermer to provide evidence for God's existence in living things.[5]

This principle basically states that what we see as an adequate cause for events in the present we assume to be an adequate cause in the past for similar events. Or, in fraud-discovery terms, *normally and regularly,* when I see things that require intelligence in the present to make, design, or create, I can, with this scientific principle, infer that similar intelligence would have been needed in the past for similar events. Let me make it easy.

When you look at Mount Rushmore and see the faces of Jefferson, Lincoln, Washington, and Roosevelt, which option best describes how they exist: plan and purpose, *or* time and random processes?[6]

Do you think that over millions of years wind, rain, and erosion carved out those four faces? Of course not, and here's why: *normally and regularly* when you see an artistic creation like Mount Rushmore, you think a intelligent designer was behind it; your everyday experience confirms this to be true. Typically, creations have creators—from something as small and simple as a street sign to the large and intricate Mount Rushmore. Denying this would be the financial equivalent of a clothes-hanger company earning 40 percent annual returns when every other hanger company barely ekes out 15 percent.

But you do not have to travel to South Dakota to confirm this principle of uniformity—you are another example. Right now, reading this book, your heart is beating. According to Philip Bishop, professor of exercise physiology at the University of Alabama,

> If you're in average physical condition, it beats between 60 and 70 times per minute, 93,000 times per day, 655,000

times per week, 34 million times per year, and 2.4 billion times in the average lifespan.

What's so amazing is that, most of the time, your heart fuels itself, paces itself, repairs itself, and alters itself in response to lifestyle changes, with no conscious effort on your part. In addition to your heart, your liver is detoxifying your blood, your brain is storing away information, cells are being formed and cells destroyed, energy is being used and produced, and many other tasks vital to life and function all carry on in a wonderful, harmonious way.[7]

Author Taylor Richardson, writing on the Apologetics Press Web site, says,

Also, in what single place can you find the following things: 19 million cells, 625 sweat glands, 90 oil glands, 65 hairs, 19 feet of blood vessels, and 19,000 sensory cells? The answer: in one square inch of human skin! The human skin is considered the largest organ in the body (about 16 percent of your body weight), and covers an area of 20 square feet. Your skin, or integument, has many different protective and metabolic functions that help keep your body stabilized.[8]

The skin provides us a sense of touch, helps regulate our body temperature, acts as a chemical processing plant for the entire body, and helps protect the inside of the body like the rubber rings around bumper cars at an amusement park.[9]

Your nervous system is also amazingly complex.

It has the ability to communicate the feel of pain resulting from intense pressure, yet adapts appropriately to the pressure of sitting or standing without distracting neural traffic. A nervous system just like yours precisely controls the muscles of the concert pianist playing Chopin, the baseball slugger making contact with a 98-mph fastball, and the gymnast performing a triple somersault to a precise landing.[10]

Now, normally and regularly, in my everyday experience when I see this kind of engineering, I think there must be an engineer! But Dr. Shermer's response to this kind of evidence is to implement the technique of *diversion*. He points to a few examples of apparent bad design, like the panda's thumb and the male nipple.[11] In our debate, my defense was that just because my Windows operating system breaks down, it does not mean that it was not created! After all, just because design can be improved upon does not mean there was no design at all.

Moreover, people a lot smarter than I am have provided more detailed, reasoned explanations to Dr. Shermer's panda's thumb and male nipple examples[12]—but the point is the use of the diversion technique. If he can just get you to think about that panda's thumb, that may divert your attention from the obvious brilliance and intricate complexity of the human brain, with its trillions of connections, or any other part of the human body—heart, nervous system, skin, and all.

My second argument is simple and deals with *disclosing material facts* about the limitations of science and statements that cannot be supported with the scientific method. During the debate and in many conversations leading up to the debate, Dr. Shermer repeatedly emphasized one point, which was "you cannot know." This is the very definition of agnosticism.

"Simply stated, a person cannot know God exists—period. We just cannot know." He said that over and over again to me before and during the debate. However, despite the many times he indicated what could *not* be known, there was one thing he did know for sure. You can bet I pointed this inconsistency out in the debate.

"Dr. Shermer says you simply cannot know. But here's what he does know for sure—God does not exist and the Bible is not true." I paused for effect and tried to allow the contradiction of his claim to not be sure about anything, yet simultaneously claiming to be sure God did not exist.

"*That* he knows for sure!" I declared in an attempt to be funny. "But he wants you here tonight to know that you "cannot know," but he knows one thing—God doesn't exist. But . . . he simply does not know. But . . . he does know one thing—God doesn't exist. But . . . he simply doesn't know. But he knows one thing—intellectually, the Bible is a joke." And so on—the crowd laughed. But let me anchor this point one step further with a personal example.

I suffer from terrible migraines. My neurologist is an awesome man and brilliant in his field. Dr. Andrew Blumenfeld is a coveted speaker on the cutting-edge technology to help migraine sufferers, which includes Botox, nerve blockers, and the latest preventative remedies. Over the last few years we have become friends; he even lets me call him Andy instead of the more formal Dr. Blumenfeld. Not long ago I went to his office to get a series of blocker shots, injections right into my head. Trust me, it is no fun, but the pain of the migraine is still far worse than a few Novocain shots to the temple.

This particular day I looked really bad. Dr. Blumenfeld took the time to console me and ask how I was doing. After a brief conversation, I asked him a basic, simple question: "Andy, can you please tell me how I can eat chocolate at four o'clock yesterday afternoon and eighteen hours later have a migraine headache so bad I need these blocker shots?"

He finished the last injection and this man, one of the nation's most respected neurologists, placed his hand on my shoulder and looked me in the eye before answering.

"You know Barry, we just don't know. We kind of know why things like MSG and nitrates [found in lunch meats] cause migraines, but frankly, we do not know the clinical answer to the chocolate question. There is so much more that we still do not know."

Here is a physician who is tops in his field, well-respected by his peers, and yet he was humble enough to concede that medical science simply does not have the answer to that question, despite billions of dollars in research and years of study. Don't get me wrong. Science and medical advancement are great stuff and I am all for them—especially when my head is pounding.

But when it comes to questions about the existence of God, why don't scientists simply disclose the material fact that they were not there to observe "Let there be light" and that nothing like it is observable or happening today. Why not just do what Dr. Blumenfeld does and disclose the material fact of limitations to science?

This led to my third argument in the debate, which was to

point out Dr. Shermer's apparent inconsistency in rejecting the miraculous while affirming *big conclusions from little evidence.* In his book, Shermer often quotes famed philosopher and skeptic David Hume,[13] who is best known for his essays that deny miracles because he feels they were "past singularities" that were not observable then nor repeatable now; therefore they're outside the realm of science. Hume said this about things like the resurrection of Jesus by stating that he could believe people die and do not rise from the dead, because that is something he sees every day—but to believe that somebody died and did rise is a past singularity that was not observed or repeated, nor does it happen in his everyday experience.

However, Dr. Shermer believes in macro evolution as stated in his book, a copy of which he personally autographed to me.[14] Yet he was not there to witness the formation of the first living cell from non life. The theory of past singularity (or macro evolution) states that at one time in the distant past, life evolved from non life, but because this theory has never been witnessed or reproduced in a laboratory, it is not repeatable. In other words, he uses the technique of drawing big conclusions from little evidence.

If you are still not convinced that the practice of this double standard still happens today, consider the example of Carl Sagan's SETI Program (Search for Extraterritorial Intelligence), which spent billions of dollars based on the notion that receiving one simple intelligent message from outer space would prove that life exists on other planets. Based on his belief, intelligent messages must have an intelligent source behind them. He was even able to convince other scientists of his theory. The irony is that these same scientists reject special creation despite multiple examples from living things of far more specified complexity and intelligence than one message from space, which never came.[14] In one convenient scenario, intelligence confirms the belief of an intelligent source (outer space). But in the other scenario, much more intelligence confirms macro evolution by random chance. That smells of fraud to me.

No matter what we may say, it is beyond the scope of this book to delve more deeply into past singularities. But I can assure you that *my* past singularity *does* have an eyewitness, and it's not an invisible elf on the top of my head. Nor do I need to employ the three fraud techniques to espouse or substantiate my view. And it's only thanks to God that I have the strength and motivation to walk the comeback trail each day. God gave me a second chance.

———

So who won the debate? The very next day Dr. Shermer posted on his Web site that he had won. You might expect a self-serving comment from me stating otherwise, but since the entire event was taped (including the questions and answers following the debate), I will let you formulate your own opinion. In fact, I'd encourage it. But on a personal level, something far more important happened that night that forever changed my life.

Not that he ever asked me to . . . and not that he needed me to, but during that debate, the God of the universe allowed me, a liar and a thief, the opportunity to use my past experiences as a fraud-perpetrating failure to formulate discussions designed to help people believe in the God of the second chance. What irony—all the while I was there defending God's existence, God had a different message, one that came through loud and clear. He wanted everyone there to know just what he could do even with the life of a failure like me!

FINAL APPLICATION

Dylan and Robert started preschool this year. For most parents this is a proud moment representing growth and progress—but not for people who are a part of the *fellowship of the failures*. And that is because it is a keen reminder to me that one day very, very soon, I will have to sit down with the two people who look up to and admire me more than anyone else in this universe and somehow explain to them that they will one day run into kids at school who will tease them about their father being a convicted felon. It's inevitable.

I have been thinking of creative ways of making this "material disclosure" with my sons. This discussion will not take place tomorrow, as they are still very young, but one day in the not-so-distant future I must confront the pain of my past. So I have worked hard on what I will tell them that day, and here is how I envision that conversation:

"Robert and Dylan, your father failed because he lied and cheated, and I cannot blame anyone but myself for those decisions. Although I may have had the best of intentions when I first went into business, I quickly learned that even though I wanted to do what was right, I was prepared to do what was wrong. So I set my feet on the path of personal compromise, and that is when my fate was sealed. After I failed and went to prison for many years, I resolved not to fail jail and identified the areas in my life that triggered my initial failure so I would not sink again.

Boys, on this road to comeback, your father has endured much criticism, and I continue to encounter people who doubt me because of the past. But I have been able to overcome these obstacles because of some "paramedics" who are a significant part of my life—people who have chosen to believe the best about me despite my past. In fact, I have learned that my past can actually be used to help people, so I have dedicated my life to doing just that through the Fraud Discovery Institute.

Robert and Dylan, what has changed most in me since my failure is how I define success. To me, success is more about giving than getting. It's more about accumulating meaningful relation-ships than the accumulation of cars, houses, and a large port-folio.

I want you boys to know that I have been on this comeback road for years now, and have learned a simple principle—truth plus time equals trust. The longer I am on this road, the more I am able to rebuild credibility with those whom I have disap-pointed in the past. It's a slow process, but the rewards are worth waiting for. I've also learned the futility of trying to prove that I am somehow good enough based on what I have accomplished.

Finally, I am convinced of the existence of the God of the second chance. I have even made him the very foundation of my comeback and am naïve enough to believe in things like miracles and life after death. So, based on that belief, I want you boys to promise me something." I will wait for them to respond.

"What is that, Daddy?" they will say.

"When I die, I want you make sure you place four words on

my tombstone. These four words will be proof to the world forever that I believe in this God and that he is the foundation of my
comeback."

"OK, Daddy. What are those four words?" they will ask.

And I will answer very simply, "Down, but not out."

NOTES

INTRODUCTION: FALLING SHORT
1. Michelle Magennis, "Abraham Lincoln–Basic Lifeline and His Failures," http://www.wiprogram.org/leadership/yl02_research_papers/old_papers/ABRAHAM_LINCOLN.htm.

STEP ONE: IT'S ALL ABOUT YOU!
1. Robert E. Kessler, "Ex-con Man Stars in Sting, Former Stock Swindler Barry Minkow, Now a Minister, Helps the FBI in the Arrest of a Man on LI Who Allegedly Ran a Phony Hedge Fund Scheme," *Newsday*, 20 April 2005, A.24.

STEP TWO: DON'T FAIL FAILURE
1. While going to graduate school I first heard this concept from Andy Stanley, senior pastor of North Point Community Church in Atlanta, Georgia. His influence on me inspired this chapter, and I give credit to him for the ideas relating to the Principle of the Path.

STEP THREE: WATCH THOSE TRIGGERS
1. "Bliss Gets Second Chance with CBA's Wizards," ESPN.com News Services, 26 August 2005, http://sports.espn.go.com/espn/news/story?id=2143887.
2. Ibid.

STEP FOUR: PREPARE FOR CRITICISM . . . AND I MEAN
REALLY PREPARE

1. "Budd Dwyer," Wikipedia, http://en.wikipedia.org/wiki/
   R._Budd_Dwyer.
2. Victoria Thomson, "Former Enron Executive's Suicide
   Note Made Public," 12 April 2002, *Scotsman*, http://
   thescotsman.scotsman.com/business.cfm?id=390692002.
3. "Donnie Moore," Wikipedia, quote attributed to Al Michaels
   of ABC-TV, http://en.wikipedia.org/wiki/Donnie_Moore.
4. "Donnie Moore," Wikipedia, http://en.wikipedia.org/wiki/
   Donnie_Moore.
5. Jay Posner, "New Leaf Turns Up on HBO Show," *San Diego
   Union-Tribune*, 12 May 2006, D.8 [Emphasis mine].
6. The company's name was deleted purposefully from this
   e-mail. This redaction in no way affects the original context or intent of the e-mail [Emphasis mine].
7. R. Geoffrey Brown, PhD, "If at First You Don't Succeed"
   (sermon transcript), Tape 37. The same information can
   also be found at "Ulysses S. Grant," http://en.wikipedia.
   org/wiki/Ulysses_S._Grant.
8. "Ulysses S. Grant: Scandals," http://www.reference.com/
   browse/wiki/Ulysses_S._Grant.

STEP FIVE: EMBRACE THOSE WHO BELIEVE IN YOU

1. Public Company Accounting Oversight Board, "Board
   Opens Fifth Regional Office" (press release), 16 August
   2004, http://www.pcaob.com/News_and_Events/News/
   2004/08-16.aspx [Emphasis mine].
2. Robert Anglen, "Charity's Investment Plan Probed,"
   Arizona Republic, 10 September 2006.

STEP SIX: YOUR BAGGAGE IS THE KEY TO YOUR COMEBACK

1. This information comes from a presentation given by Ravi
   Zacharias, in which I remember him telling the story of
   John De Lorean.

2. Warren Bennis and Burt Nanus, *Leaders: Strategies for Taking Charge* (Harper and Row, 1986) 70.

STEP SEVEN: REDEFINE WHAT A WIN IN LIFE REALLY LOOKS LIKE

1. Mark 8:36 (NKJV). The New King James Version®, copyright 1979, 1980, 1982, by Thomas Nelson, Inc., Publishers, Nashville, Tennessee.
2. Matthew Heller, "Death and Denial at Herbalife: The Untold Story of Mark Hughes' Public Image, Secret Vice and Tragic Destiny," *Los Angeles Times*, 18 February 2001. I had the privilege of meeting Mr. Heller in March of 2004 when he wrote an article about me for the *Los Angeles Times* magazine (published in May of 2004).
3. Ibid.
4. Ibid.
5. Rick Reilly, "A Paragon Rising above the Madness" *Sports Illustrated*, 14 March 2000.
6. Gary L. Thomas, *Devotions for a Sacred Marriage* (Zondervan, 2005), 28–30.
7. Reilly, "A Paragon Rising above the Madness."

STEP EIGHT: TRUTH + TIME = TRUST

1. More about this will be discussed in step ten.
2. I realize this is neither a scientific conclusion nor an exhaustive study on the Second Law. But that it does teach this is confirmed in *When Skeptics Ask* by Dr. Norman Geisler and Ron Brooks (Baker Book House, 1990) on page 220, where the actual quote is: "Everything is tending toward disorder and the universe is running down."
3. Richard Wilner, "Rainmaker Shoots Off a Vengeful E-mail," *New York Post*, 28 August 2005, 29.
4. "Stormpays Good Honest Man, Barry Minkow" (individual message board post), Talkgold HYIP Investment Forum, 29 March 2006, http://www.talkgold.com/forum/ r85188-.

html. Abridged for my purposes.

5. Mark Maremont, "SEC Alleges Internet Ponzi Scheme," *Wall Street Journal,* 27 February 2006.

STEP NINE: YOU ARE GOOD ENOUGH!

1. Peter Scazzero, *Emotionally Healthy Spirituality* (Integrity Publishing, 2006), 15–16.

2. Ibid.

3. John Maxwell audio lecture, "Creation Day 5: Genesis 1:20–23," from the series "The Battle for the Beginning," transcript available at http://www.gty.org/resources.php? section=transcripts&aid=215993.

STEP TEN: BUILD FROM A NEW FOUNDATION

1. Max Lucado, *Next Door Savior,* (W Publishing Group, 2003).

2. Michael Shermer, *Why People Believe Weird Things: Pseudoscience, Superstition, and Other Confusions of Our Time* (W.H. Freeman & Company, 1998).

3. Shermer, *Why People Believe Weird Things,* 214.

4. Just for the sake of thoroughness, another great question to ask is why would anyone who can earn 40 percent annual returns need to raise money? After all, if the company has a vehicle by which it can earn 40 percent a year, its own money would double in less than three years, which, as you see, begs the obvious question—why would they need to raise any money at all?

5. I first learned about this principle from Dr. Norman Geisler when I was in graduate school. He has since written about it in many of his books, including *When Skeptics Ask* (Baker Book House, 1995), 213–214.

6. Medical researcher and physician Dr. Michael Girouard taught me these specific examples in graduate school while I was studying several of his presentations given at a seminar.

7. Phillip Bishop, "Evidence of God in Human Physiology—Fearfully and Wonderfully Made," Leadership U (Christian Leadership Ministries), http://www.leaderu.com/science/bishop.html.

8. Taylor Richardson, "The Human Skin—Engineered by God," ApologeticsPress.org (Apologetics Press, 2004), http://www.apologeticspress.org/articles/2581.

9. Ibid.

10. Bishop, "Evidence of God."

11. Shermer, *Why People Believe Weird Things,* 146.

12. For examples, see http://www.godandscience.org/evolution/designgonebad.html.

13. Shermer, *Why People Believe Weird Things,* 45–46.

14. The SETI illustration comes from Dr. Norman Geisler's DVD series titled *False Gods of our Time,* Jeremiah Films "Miracles."

ACKNOWLEDGMENTS

To me, the greatest sin as a writer is to bore people. I hold to a very simple principle when I write and that is if I am bored while writing it, you will be bored reading it. That is why my approach with this book is unique in that I avoid the text-book, term-paper feel and rather appeal to a principle I learned in graduate school. One of my professors once said, *"All great teachers know one thing—truth is most powerful when people have to work to discover it. Truth discovered is more powerful than truth presented."*

It is for this reason that I have written this book, not as you might expect based on other "Steps to Whatever" books you may have read, but rather I have attempted to utilize illustration and personal experience from my life and the lives of others who have greatly impacted me to anchor each of the ten steps to coming back from failure and rebuilding your life and your career. I have always believed that illustration best leads to application.

Moreover, in almost every circumstance I have dared to use the real names, times, and locations of the events in an attempt to impute credibility to the illustrations I site. However, I have purposely avoided long quotes, multiple citations or any other literary style that resembles a term paper. And in the interest of full disclosure, I am not inerrant, so if I have misquoted a phrase or reference or made any other mistake, I ask for your forgiveness.

There is also something else that needs to be disclosed. Although my name is on the cover of the book, others have worked tirelessly behind the scenes. First, there are the usual players like my editor, Erin Hattenburg, who has the daunting task of taking each chapter after I write and making sure sentence structure and grammar rules have been applied. Let me assure you that in most cases they have not, which makes her job difficult.

Then there is Joel Miller, the Associate Publisher at Nelson Current who, despite me getting off track at least a dozen times on this project, kept me grounded and encouraged. The same can be said for Editor Alice Sullivan at Nelson Current, who was assigned to this project and simply made it better. David Dunham and Ted Squires are also worth noting. David cast the vision for this book at Jeri's Deli in Studio City and never stopped believing in this project. Ted Squires did what he always does—pulled for the guy whom he first believed in when I got out of prison in 1995 and demanded that I write a road map for others in similar situations.

Jeff Teitelman, a friend and someone I respect helped me gather valuable research for this book several months before I wrote the first chapter. And of course, there is Mel Berger, my agent at the William Morris Agency, whose work ethic and inspiration are contagious. Then, there is my wife, Lisa, who suffered through many "Honey, take care of the kids I've got to write" moments and never complained. Not once. I dedicate this book to her because she truly is my wife, helpmate, partner, and best friend.

Finally, for all of us who have failed, I want you to take courage and hope. You and I have a unique bond, which I call "fellowship of the failures." It simply means you are not alone on this road to comeback. And never forget, I'm pulling for you all the way, through each step—and if a mess-up like me can come back despite all the evil I have done, the sky is the limit for you!